ALBERTA RDSP EDITION

safe and secure

PLAN Institute for Caring Citizenship

PLAN – Planned Lifetime Advocacy Network

260 – 3665 Kingsway

Vancouver, B.C. V5R 5W2

PHONE 604 439-9566   FAX 604 439-7001

www.aletmanski.com www.planinstitute.ca www.PLAN.ca www.tyze.ca

This book uses the term "disability" to refer to those challenges, conditions, circumstances, handicaps, and impairments that may limit the functional ability of people. In all of PLAN and PLAN Institute's work, the person is the primary focus, the disability is secondary.

Library and Archives Canada Cataloguing in Publication

Etmanski, Al, 1947-

Safe and secure: six steps to creating a good life for people with disabilities /
Al Etmanski; with Jack Collins and Vickie Cammack; — Revised Alberta RDSP
edition includes bibliographical references.

ISBN 978-0-9730383-6-1

1. People with disabilities-Family relationships. 2. People with disabilities-
Finance, Personal. 3. Estate planning
Alberta. I. Collins, Jack, 1929- II. Cammack, Vickie, 1951- III. Plan Institute for
Caring Citizenship IV. Title.

HV1559.C3E8472011   C2011- 904334-3

Design and production by www.workingdesign.net

Editing services by Linda McDaniel: lmcdaniel@shaw.ca

safe and secure

SIX STEPS TO CREATING
A GOOD LIFE FOR PEOPLE
WITH DISABILITIES

Al Etmanski
with Jack Collins and Vickie Cammack

ALBERTA RDSP EDITION 2011

Acknowledgements

When there is a perfect storm of vision, passion, creativity, and commitment, something striking can happen. The families in British Columbia who started PLAN began this journey. Without their remarkable efforts, this book and the work of all the Alberta PLAN Affiliates would not have been possible. Thank you to Jack Collins, Vickie Cammack, and Al Etmanski for their vision, inspiration, and leadership.

The Alberta RDSP Edition of *Safe and Secure* is made easier by the support, insight, and voices of so many. Firstly, we acknowledge the vision and continued legacy of Tom Cain. We also thank Guy McNab. His ability to clearly explain the law and complex legal terms will make it much easier for Alberta families to begin the work that needs to be done. And to Jack Styan, Managing Director of the RDSP Resource Centre, a special thanks for lending his expertise to the technical aspects of the RDSP in Step 5.

The compassion and personal insights in this book are directly reflected in the stories you'll read. It is those personal stories that provide the breath that gives life to this book. In particular, we thank Bruce, Flora, and Maggie MacKay; Barbara, Robert, and Andrew Nish; Rod and Christel Makishi; Julia and Bethany Flumerfelt; Christian Bayus; Karin and Val Hazle; Cathy and Wayne Warren; and Betty Hahn-Sidor.

A special thank you to Linda McDaniel, whose editorial expertise assisted in keeping us on track. She inspired us to keep moving forward. Her help in coordinating the details and walking us through all the steps was immeasurable.

We extend an enormous thank you to the Alberta Law Foundation. Through their generous financial support for this edition, they have shared their commitment to informing families about the importance of future planning for their relatives with disabilities. By supporting this project, they have made a real difference in the lives of many Albertans.

Lastly but certainly not least, thank you to all of the Alberta PLAN Affiliates. Their contributions have helped to ensure that this edition of *Safe and Secure* reflects the experiences of families from across Alberta.

Dave Lawson

Executive Director LACL

Lori Litke

PLAN Coordinator LACL

> Family is who loves you.
>
> WAYSON CHOY

Introduction

We live in interesting times. We connect and are connected with each other in ways that are beyond what we could have ever imagined just a few years ago. Our connections with those around us give us a sense of belonging and the ability to contribute to something greater.

The rapid advances in technology and digital media brings social networking and connectedness to new highs and sometimes lows. We certainly can access information faster and connect easier but the depth and authenticity of connectedness and information can be uncertain.

Technology has provided us with a wider opening to our funnel in making connections and cultivating welcoming, caring communities but it is ultimately our face-to-face conversations that get the real work done.

The Alberta RDSP Edition of *Safe and Secure* is designed to help families create a good life for their relatives with disabilities. The desire to create a good life is driven by the deep conviction that every person has something meaningful and important to contribute to society.

Our communities and the sense of belonging and engagement that comes from citizenship are the basis of that good life. This book will help you build a solid foundation for your hopes and dreams and will help you share your plan for your relative's future with those who will assist.

The Federal Government's introduction of the Registered Disability Savings Plan (RDSP) has not only provided people with an excellent long-term savings vehicle, it also demonstrates a new perspective on the potential for people with disabilities to contribute to our communities. When families have a plan for the future, they can invite services in to support that plan where needed while cultivating other meaningful connections.

This Alberta RDSP Edition will go a long way to inspire and inform those that know they have an obligation that comes from deep within.

> Hope means to keep living amid desperation and to keep humming in the darkness. In the midst of a gale at sea, is to discover land in the eyes of another. It is to see that they understand you .
>
> HENRI NOUWEN

Your obligation is not just for your relative but to the whole community that would be poorer without the important and authentic contribution of your family member. The well-being of others leads to the well-being of community.

VAL HAZLE, PLAN Calgary

MELONEY PATTERSON-GILLAN, PLAN Edmonton

DAVE LAWSON, Lethridge Association for Community Living (LACL)

Contents

My Life

People make assumptions. They don't know that life as me can be rich and full and fun and, dare I say it, happy. I like my life. Can you believe that?

I know lots of people — my workers, family, friends — and they all care about me. I know that they all like me too. They like to be with me because I am fun to be with. I help people see what is really important in life — and that's connection.

I am lucky. No one expects anything of me. It's like being given an ideal life for inner exploration.

We live in such a "doing" society that we automatically pity someone with a disability because they can't "do" in the same way, instead of seeing the inner benefits. Just because you can't do, can't work, don't have a career, doesn't mean to say you're not valuable.

I think this gets back to who we are essentially without all the labels. I mean, who are you or anyone without their professions, their possessions, house, car, money, talent, etc? Stripped of everything, who are you?

KIRSTEEN MAIN

Introduction

Love is not enough

There are at least two emotions that inspired you to pick up this book. The first is love. The second is fear. We know this because we experience them too, as do the hundreds of families who have relatives with disabilities we have met over the years. You are definitely not alone.

Like everyone else, you want to die with your affairs in order. You want to leave a clear blueprint of your wishes for your relatives. At a time of great emotional stress—your death—you want to minimize the trauma. You also want to provide a secure future for those who survive you, particularly your relative with a disability.

That's the voice of love speaking.

Nevertheless, over 50 per cent of Canadians die without a Will. Most of the other 50 per cent haven't had their Will reviewed and updated for at least five years. And surprisingly, over 90 per cent of all business owners in North America die without a viable estate plan.

That's the voice of fear speaking.

So let's get right down to it. In matters of future planning, love is not enough. That's one of the main reasons this book has been written. We want to do three things:

1. We want to inspire and challenge you:
   - to begin and complete the future planning process for your relative
   - to conquer your fears
   - to replace *fear* of the future with *faith* in the future.

2. We want to guide you through the process of creating a Personal Future Plan for your relative with a disability. We want to expand your vision of the possibilities and to help you put them into concrete terms.

3. Finally, we want to shed light on the legal/financial/technical solutions available to assist you to carry out your last wishes, and to share practical tips on how to apply these solutions to your unique circumstances.

> I don't think intelligence exists without love. Love is intelligence. What kind of intelligence would you have without love?
>
> ROBIN BLASER

What we believe

We believe in families. We believe in your initiative, your dedication, your creativity, your tenacity, and your commitment. We believe that your wishes, dreams, and desires for your relative can shape the future. We believe in a world of possibilities. We believe that if you are willing to commit to the process of future planning outlined in this book, then that vision is the future your relative will have.

This book allows you to look over the shoulders of other families who are on the same journey. In this book, you will meet people who are breathing life into their dreams right now and giving shape to a brighter future for themselves and for their relatives with disabilities. While the details of their plans may be different, the issues they are confronting are remarkably similar to yours.

Another belief of ours is that this book can help. It will provide you with an overview of the whole future planning process. There are no single answers, no single solutions, and no miracles. In fact, some of the solutions will never look perfect. A Personal Future Plan is just a mixture of old-fashioned common sense, commitment, hard work, and a dash of bravado.

So enjoy, create, laugh, and cry.

Developing a Personal Future Plan –
Six steps to a safe and secure future

Many of us never really take the time to sit down and discuss what our future intentions are for our relative with a disability. Nevertheless it does come up. Maybe it pops up when you are driving home from a family gathering. Maybe one of your children mentions something in passing, but the topic quickly changes. Maybe you wake up in the middle of the night and decide it's time to talk about it in the morning. But then you don't.

> We still need dreams as adults. It amazes me how many people either deny themselves this experience or are so tied to the reality of survival that they fail to grasp the importance of being able to dream. We're talking conscious dreaming here as opposed to what occurs when we are asleep, although the two may be linked subconsciously.
>
> ROBERTA BONDAR

So many thoughts, ideas, worries, and concerns go rolling around in your head. You can hardly remember them all. How could you expect someone else to? There are so many confusing messages and countless pieces of advice, and so many complications. The need for resolution lurks just beneath the surface, emerging at the most unexpected times.

Sound familiar? That's our experience, too. Virtually all of the families we have worked with have encountered the seemingly overwhelming bits and pieces of advice and action required to prepare for the future.

Our work with families has convinced us that the process is not as complicated as it first appears. Further, we are convinced there are only a few key elements you need to focus on. We have combined these elements into what we call a Personal Future Plan. That is what this book is about. It is what we advise you to develop for your relative. But really, you will be developing it for yourself.

A Personal Future Plan is a six-step process families can follow to create a safe, secure and pleasant future for their relatives with disabilities. It includes the best of your experiences, your dreams and nightmares, your wishes for the future, and your knowledge and expertise. It combines all of these with the active involvement of your relative with a disability, other members of your family, and selected knowledgeable professionals.

It is a plan that you create, control, and direct. It is focused on the here and now. It is also geared to a time when you will no longer be around.

The six steps are as follows:

Step one	Clarifying your vision
Step two	Nurturing friendship
Step three	Creating a home
Step four	Making sound decisions
Step five	Achieving financial security
Step six	Securing your plan

> Community is where "we" become "us."
>
> TIM BRODHEAD

Advice for parents of younger children

As you will discover, in addition to Maggie's story sprinkled throughout the six steps, there are a number of sections in this book specifically written for parents who have children under the age of 18.

Parents with younger children are faced with enough daunting challenges: being first time parents, dealing with the news of a child's disability, and responding to additional health challenges. We know this can be a tumultuous and intense period. You may not wish to focus on the future. We understand. Here are some tips to help you along the way:

- Grandparents can help in a variety of ways, including making contributions to your child's RDSP.
  NOTE There is a danger that the generosity of a grandparent in setting up a trust (either discretionary or non-discretionary) for a grandchild may result in that grandchild's AISH benefits being eliminated. Grandparents should be cautioned to thoroughly discuss this eventuality with both their lawyer and the parents of the grandchild that they are intending to "benefit" before creating any trust.
- Life insurance can be an affordable way to finance a trust. You control the monthly payments and, should you die, the proceeds finance a discretionary trust for your child.
- Don't hesitate to invite friends into your child's life. Keep track of every person who is a friend with your child. You will be pleasantly surprised at how many of these people will become Personal Network members when the time comes.
- Before high school is a good time to begin organizing a social network for your teenage child.
- Remember to create a Will and indicate who you want to become guardian of your children. Step Five outlines what happens if you don't.
- Connecting with other parents who have children with disabilities is the single best support for any of the tough decisions you will have to make on behalf of your child.

How to use this book

We suggest you skim through this book until you come to a section that you'd like to work on. Once you've decided to focus on one section, answer all the questions and complete all the worksheets. If you don't want to mark up the book— and most don't—you can download the worksheets from www.lacl.ca. Click on *Safe and Secure* Worksheets.

You'll be surprised how the questions in one section will lead directly into the concerns of another section. Each one informs and guides the other. Before you know it, your planning will be complete and you'll have a record of your intentions, all contained in one place.

This book allows you to be an informed consumer of the professional services that are available in the future planning industry. By following the steps and advice presented here, you will be better prepared, use less professional time, and save yourself money.

We invite you to customize this book to your needs. Add your own personal data, photos, records, medical information, and so on. Keep this book in a safe place. You should never underestimate how valuable this information will be to your survivors.

Think of *Safe and Secure* as your manuscript for the future.

clarifying
your vision

I am a sailor in my dreams
I travel from land to land
My heart is a compass
I will never be lost.

LIZ ETMANSKI

Maggie the teacher

The journey begins with a father looking back

WHEN MAGGIE was only three months old, she required surgery to repair two small holes in her heart. That time was a blur for us. We were worried that our little girl wasn't thriving and growing because her heart wasn't pumping efficiently.

We worried about the surgery, of course. How could the doctors work on such a small little heart? And we worried about recovery when it was all over and we were back at home. Was she growing as much as she should? Would she ever develop the muscle strength to suck from a bottle?

I didn't know what to expect. What kind of life would Maggie live? What opportunities would she have? What barriers would she face?

After Maggie was safely through the medical challenges of the first few years, I got connected to the Lethbridge Association for Community Living (LACL) and I began to learn that there were many other parents and families who were on a similar journey to ours. And I learned there were many who had gone before us.

Through our involvement with LACL, we learned about PLAN, an organization with similar values but looking at what to do and how to plan for the later years of life, both for parents and for their sons and daughters with disabilities. Although Maggie was still very young—now an incredibly cute and busy toddler—it seemed to me that it was a good time to begin thinking about what the future would look like and to learn about concerns and potential solutions for that stage in our lives.

It is as important for us, Maggie's parents, to be connected to others in the community as it is for Maggie to be connected to her friends and peers. We learn so much from those who have gone before. Their wisdom and experience can only make life better for us and therefore Maggie. ∎

BRUCE AND FLORA MACKAY
as told by Bruce Mackay

Clarifying your vision

Remember the old saying: If you don't know where you are going, any road will get you there? Well, we think it's true. That's why, as you begin planning for the future, you need to be clear about what you want. What are you trying to achieve for your relative? What do you imagine for their future? What are your goals? What do you want to prevent? What do you want to maintain? What do you want people to know when they gather to discuss your wishes after you are gone?

Without specific answers to these questions, the rest of your planning will be cloudy and incomplete. Knowing what you want to achieve is the first step in creating a Personal Future Plan.

For most of us, the obvious place to start is by completing our Will and establishing a trust for our relative.

Most of the planning time should be spent identifying what you are trying to achieve, thinking through your goals and objectives, and clarifying your vision. Once these steps become clear, you will be in a better position to evaluate the various options available. Then the technical solutions such as increasing the value of your estate, choosing your trustee(s), and finding the precise legal clauses will follow. Then—and only then—should you seek the advice of professionals. Your Will and estate plan will be more relevant and useful because your directions are clear.

Think of your last plane ride. Did you ask the pilot where you should go? Of course not. You made that decision first. Then you examined the scheduling options and made your decision about price and so on. That's the most effective way to utilize the services of Will and estate planning professionals. It saves them time and you money.

Cathy's caring network

CATHY HAS BEEN a Lifetime Member of PLAN Edmonton for three years. Her network gatherings have included family, people from church, and the community. The network is still growing and network members are committed to being there for Cathy's future.

Cathy is a caring individual who likes to help others. She also loves children and pets. She lives and works in St. Albert and has shared a house with two other women for the past 11 years. These roommates have become the best of friends. Cathy cooks, bakes, and does crafts with them.

Cathy keeps very busy by regularly going to the gym, the swimming pool, and the bowling lanes. She also goes dancing, to the movies, the library, and out for coffee dates. Her network plays a key role in facilitating many of these activities.

Cathy is both well-liked and appreciated as a volunteer at Parents' Place Day Care and the Youville Home Care Facility.

She keeps very involved with church activities including two events called Friendship Club and Faith and Light. She also enjoys singing.

She is working on improving her reading and writing with one of the network members who is tutoring her.

At the top of Cathy's wish list for her future is to have a female shopping companion so she doesn't have to rely on her brothers and her Dad. This is one of the many things she misses about her Mom who passed away five years ago.

WAYNE WARREN (Cathy's brother)

What is a personal future plan?

A Personal Future Plan is a written summary of your plans for the social and financial well-being of your family member with a disability.

We have learned that the most effective question when making a Personal Future Plan is: What is a good life? Families tell us that a good life for their relative should include the following elements:

- caring and loving relationships
- a place of one's own
- choice
- contribution
- financial security.

The worksheets at the end of each chapter will assist you with answering this question for your family's unique circumstances. To download a copy, please visit www.lacl.ca and click on the *Safe and Secure* Worksheets.

What is a vision?

Visions are creations of the heart as well as of the mind. A vision is your description of a desired future for your relative. A vision is about passion—your passion for the future economic and social well-being of your relative. That's why it is so important to address dreams as well as nightmares. Fears, worries, hopes, and dreams are all keys to unlocked passion.

A clearly written statement of your vision will help focus your attention. Since a vision reflects your values, your traditions, and your family history, it creates a context for the other components of your Personal Future Plan.

Clarifying and sharing your vision of a desired future for your relative:
- enables you to see the world through your relative's eyes
- invites the involvement of other members of the family
- encourages others to better understand what is involved and gets them thinking as to how they can help
- brings preferred and desirable scenarios into the open
- suggests new opportunities
- moves you forward
- changes the present.

> The fundamental job of the imagination in ordinary life is to produce out of the society we have to live in, a vision of the society we want to live in.
>
> NORTHROP FRYE

If music be the food of love, play on

GARLAND COHEN was in her eighties when she and her son David joined PLAN Vancouver. She had been pushing the future to the back of her mind for a long time, hoping for a miracle. Garland wasn't afraid of dying; she was afraid of leaving David alone.

David had an apartment in the basement of the house where he and his mother lived for 20 years. While he knew many people in the community, none of them knew one another. Garland's health was failing and she feared that David was growing increasingly isolated and might slip through the cracks.

With the help of PLAN, Garland set up a trust and started a network for David. Soon after, she was diagnosed with cancer. David's network provided the support she needed to die at home. After she passed away, the network helped David move into an apartment of his own.

In the years since Garland's death, David has said that the network gave him a sense of security about living in the community, and that he didn't feel alone. Over time, the network helped him tackle issues like employment, using computers, and going back to school. "They're very wonderful people," he said of his friends, and they said the same about him. John Meyer, an early network member and advisor to Garland in setting up a trust for David more than 12 years ago, observed that if Garland could see how David has thrived, "She'd be tickled pink."

•

At the age of 61, when David was diagnosed with brain cancer, his friends rallied round. Weeks later, on a December evening, he and more than 75 others gathered in a room filled with Christmas cheer to celebrate his extraordinary life.

David's dedicated patronage of the musical arts was evident among the guests. Canada's first lady of opera, Judith Forst, related how, for decades, David had been coming back stage after every performance to compliment her. "When David loves something," she said, "it isn't 50 percent, it's 100 percent." Linda Lee Thomas, lead pianist with the Vancouver Symphony Orchestra, said, "A concert of the VSO is not complete without David Cohen. He comes back stage and always has that wonderful hand extended and shares his generous thanks."

David was also well known in political circles. He inherited his mother's passion for peace and social justice, and his letter writing for Amnesty International is legendary. During civic elections, David volunteered his time and rarely missed a local political

continued on page 24

We have learned that sharing your ideas—particularly when you put them in writing—is important. Since you won't be around, it is better to begin the discussion with your other children, extended family, friends, and potential supporters now. Relying on others without telling them could create problems for everyone.

You don't want to assume—as one Mom did—that her other children knew and understood the complete medical background of her son, only to find that they were too busy growing up to notice, let alone to make notes! Or a Dad who told us that he intends to rely on his next-door neighbours to carry out his wishes for his daughter, without determining first whether they are interested in discussing any of the details with him.

So what are we afraid of?

What keeps so many of us from even thinking about the future let alone formalizing our future wishes for our survivors? What causes our paralysis? Why don't we act? Maybe it's fear.

Love and fear are two sides of the same coin. The coin is called passion. The word, passion, stems from the Latin word for suffering. Wouldn't you agree that suffering is a mixture of love and fear?

Fear is an intriguing emotion. Fear distorts our perception and confuses us about what is going on and about what is possible. When we use words like *can't, ought to, if only, doubt,* and *impossible*, we are under the influence of fear. Fear draws a dark and cold curtain between our intentions and our actions. Like a schoolyard bully, its appearance is deceiving. It's actually more imposing in our minds than in reality.

In our own personal struggles with the issues of future planning and in our work with families, we can identify three schoolyard bullies that everyone must find the courage to confront. We offer them here because we believe that where there is clarity, there is comfort. Where there is understanding, there is the ability to change.

FEAR OF OPENING UP Sharing your hopes and worries means discussing intensely personal matters with others—our spouse, family members, friends or acquaintances, and professionals. This may be awkward. We may need to contact people who have never

If music be...

continued from page 22

meeting. At the party for David, Vancouver mayoral candidate Jim Green—out of the country at the time—sent a letter recalling how David's presentation on a panel about the opera, *Of Mice and Men,* moved a tenor in attendance to tears.

Others spoke of David's kindness, the thoughtful way he thanks people, and his generous spirit. Lyle Lexier, a member of David's network, said, "David Cohen has been my friend for 15 years. We talk about opera and human rights and the release of political prisoners and how to end capital punishment." Longtime friend Owen Underhill disclosed, "I don't think I've ever felt so affirmed in my life as when David left me a telephone message about my work as a composer, a conductor, a father, and a friend."

Network member Barrie Vickers spoke for everyone in the room when he addressed the guest of honour, "It is a wonderful gift you have given us David, and we'll live out the joy that you've given to us."

When David took the microphone, he said, "Thank you for your beautiful words." Then the whole room joined in a rousing verse of Hark the Herald Angels Sing. A long line formed at David's side, and for the next hour he graciously greeted friend after friend.

SANDRA SHIELDS

Post Script

David Cohen passed away peacefully and surrounded by friends. Some of his friends smile in relating how very fitting that the end of David's life should fall on Mozart's birthday—amid magnificent musical tributes. PLAN Vancouver staff shall miss David's daily phone calls that kept everyone up to date on current events and local performing arts schedules. As one of the people on David's network remarked, "He had a good life and a good ending. Really, what more could anyone ask for?"

demonstrated any interest in our relative. Or we may not know who to turn to or who to trust. And we risk rejection.

We've grown up believing in self-sufficiency. We've taken our responsibilities seriously. We've tried all our lives to make sure others wouldn't have to shoulder our responsibilities. We've done the best we can.

With future planning we have to share our hopes, our dreams, our fears, and our anxieties with others. We need to ask others to:

- help us with our planning
- carry out our wishes after we are gone
- believe in our relative and the possibilities for their future.

To do this, we need to reach out. We need to know who we can rely on. After all, what good are your plans if no one else knows about them? Sure, they could read about your wishes in your Will. But will the readers get the complete picture? Will they know what you really want? What if they have questions? Maybe they aren't interested? How can you be sure you will be understood?

FEAR OF DEATH Death is not a popular topic in our society. Even a cursory look at the popular media suggests that our culture is obsessed with youth, living forever, and avoiding sickness and infirmity. An illusion is offered: We can cheat death. While it may not be stated, the implicit message is that diet, exercise, and medical intervention will keep us forever young or forever alive. As Margaret Mead said of our culture, "When people are born we rejoice, and when they're married we celebrate, but when they die we try to pretend nothing has happened."

The fear of death is there for all of us. It lurks just beneath the surface, never quite deep enough, though, to be ignored. Perhaps it presents itself as anxiety, perhaps as an awful sense of impermanence, perhaps as loneliness. We may harbour the belief that parents who have sons and daughters without disabilities have fewer anxieties about death than we do. Not true. Perhaps what separates us from those parents is our need to address the future of our relatives not just for our lifetime, but for their lifetime.

Life is full of dying; life is full of death. When the reality of death strikes, it reminds us of our physical limitations, and of the depth of our spirit. We may have regrets and yet be thankful that we have a new beginning, an awareness that while we are in the shadow of death, a new life has begun.

DAVID KUHL, M.D.

> Statistically, 100% of the shots you don't take don't go in.
>
> WAYNE GRETZKY

For younger people, death can feel very remote. Even thinking about it seems perverse. But death is inevitable and is a natural part of life which we all have to face sooner or later. The Dalai Lama says there are two ways we can choose to deal with the prospect of our death: we can ignore it or we can confront it. Confronting and accepting our own mortality spurs us into action. We gain the wisdom to accept the inevitable and the knowledge to realize that it's better for everyone if we think about and, as importantly, begin to organize our affairs.

FEAR OF MAKING A MISTAKE, OR FEAR OF NOT BEING PERFECT

Now here's an irony for you. In thinking about the future, many of us feel we need to create the "perfect" plan. We are afraid that we haven't covered all the bases. Somehow we think we can make the future perfect even though the day-to-day doesn't always turn out the way we planned.

According to financial and estate planners, lawyers, accountants, and everyone else involved in the future planning business, the most common excuse for not making a Will is the fear of not getting it right. Indecision can paralyze even those with the best intentions. In trying to make perfect decisions, we risk indefinite delay. Perfection equals postponement. Doing our best is as perfect as it will ever get.

Our own collection of top ten reasons for NOT preparing for your future

1. The future is uncertain. Better eat dessert first. SARAH LEE
2. I'm afraid that if I make a Will, I will die. JOE AVERAGE
3. I never think of the future. It comes soon enough. EINSTEIN
4. I'm not afraid to die. I just don't want to be there when it happens. WOODY ALLEN
5. I don't see any dark clouds on the horizon. There's nothing to worry about.
   GENERAL CUSTER, U.S. CAVALRY
6. I've developed a new philosophy—I only dread one day at a time.
   CHARLES M. SCHULZ, PEANUTS
7. Dying is a very dull and dreary affair. I intend to have nothing to do with it. SOMERSET MAUGHAM
8. The future is not what it used to be. PAUL VALERY
9. I have seen the future and it doesn't work. ROBERT FULFORD
10. The future is made of the same stuff as the present. SIMONE WEIL

Thoughts on putting it off

- We're not in crisis yet. We still have loads of time.
- The process is too costly, both financially and emotionally.
- I don't know who to turn to. My community of support is too small.
- I'm worn out from too many previous battles. I just need a break.
- We're still young.
- The future is too hard to contemplate.
- I'm a procrastinator. I have a reputation to live up to.

Plans evolve

Personal Future Plans will change as circumstances change. It takes time for your dreams to evolve. You can always update and revise your Future Plan. In fact, you should expect to make changes along the way. We all get wiser as we get older, don't we? You can expect to gain insight and pick up tips.

Who among us can predict the future? Can we anticipate all eventualities? Here's a simple exercise: Place yourself twenty years in the past. Would you have predicted Barack Obama as President of the United States? The threat of global warming? The careers of your children? The size of your nest egg?

To put it another way: have you ever made a decision without having all the answers? Would Columbus have set sail? Would Mother Teresa have moved to the slums of Calcutta? The truth is that we often have to proceed as best we can without all the answers. Hindsight is the only guarantee of perfect vision.

Reflections on having a personal future plan

- It's fair to other family members. They now know what's going on.
- My worries about outside interference are gone.
- I'm better prepared to face the unknown.
- I've done the best I can.
- I've left a legacy of love.
- I'm at peace.

I Am Me

Watching, always watching,

People just pass by.

Oh, they notice alright,

But what they see is not me.

They see a wheelchair,

They see a body that to them is hopeless

They see a body, and then they say, "Oh, poor thing."

They, society, have not seen me.

I am a person who thinks, feels and lives.

I am a writer.

I am a student.

And when given a chance, I am a friend.

I am a person like you.

I cry, laugh and get mad.

True, I do need some extra help but I am still a person.

When you look at me, look at the person.

I am not a wheelchair.

I am not handicapped.

And I am not an object for display.

I AM A PERSON.

I AM ME.

KIRSTEEN MAIN

Worksheet 1

After you're gone: clarifying your vision

It's the day after your death. Describe what a safe and secure life will look like for your relative.

_____

List ten words to describe a typical day for your relative, in the best of all possible worlds.

_____

Use some key words to describe your worst nightmare for your relative after you're gone.

_____

What is the most important message you want to leave your relative with a disability? _____

_____

What do you want your survivors to help with after you've gone? _____

_____

When your executors/trustees meet, what do you want them to do first? _____

_____

What are the three priorities you want future caregivers to remember about your relative?

1. _____

2. _____

3. _____

What are the important arrangements you've made to ensure a good life for your relative?_____

_____

How do you want to be remembered by your relative? _____

_____

Worksheet 2

A family portrait

Use this worksheet to develop a portrait of your relative as it will be an important record to pass on to your survivors.

Health

List names of current doctors, specialists, and health practitioners: _____

_____

List current health concerns: _____

_____

List current health treatments: _____

_____

List current health precautions and alternatives: _____

_____

Briefly describe key features of your relative's medical history: _____

_____

Education and work

List your relative's current educational and/or work activity: _____

_____

What are their future dreams in this area? What other possibilities would they like to explore?

_____

What are some highlights from your relative's school experience? What did they like about it?
What didn't they like about it? _____

_____

Who are the people from the past that your relative would like to connect with?

_____

Who are the people with whom your relative still has a close connection with?

_____

What are some highlights of your relative's work experience? What did they like about it? What
didn't they like about it? _____

_____

Housing

Describe your relative's current living arrangements:_____

_____

What are some future housing options/possibilities for your relative? _____

_____

Summarize their previous living arrangements:_____

_____

What did your relative like about them, dislike about them? _____

_____

Who are the people who had a significant relationship with your relative in these previous living arrangements?_____

_____

Leisure and recreation

List your relative's current social, recreational, cultural, artistic, and athletic activities: _____

_____

What are your relative's interests and preferred activities in these areas?_____

_____

What are some future possibilities in the area of leisure and recreation?_____

_____

What does your relative most like to do? _____

_____

Personal

How would you describe your relative's beliefs and values? _____

_____

What customs and traditions are important in your family? _____

_____

Is spiritual and religious worship important for your relative? Is this an area that could be
explored further?_____

_____

What are (or will be) the significant events, markers, or milestones in your relative's life? _____

_____

What brings comfort and peace to your relative? _____

_____

Who has been your relative's greatest source of emotional support other than yourself? _____

_____

What does your relative gain the most pleasure from? _____

_____

Who are the most significant people in your relative's life?_____

_____

What are your relative's favourite possessions? _____

_____

Worksheet 3

A letter to the future

The last wishes of family members are honoured and respected in our society.

A letter to the future is your opportunity to tell your survivors how you would like to be remembered, and how you would like your relative with a disability to be cared for.

This is not an easy letter to write. Think of it as the letter you might write in the middle of the night when you can't sleep. Be frank about your hopes and fears. Tell those who will survive you what's most important to you.

Dear _____,

With love,

nurturing friendship

We spend our free time with friends. We can relax with them and allow our masks to fall. It is all right to be ourselves and we can do what we like, we are not constrained by rules.

But friendship also implies commitment. A true friend feels responsible for his friends, during bad times as well as good, in success and failure, humiliation and sorrow.

JEAN VANIER

Maggie the teacher

The lesson of friendship

ONLY A GENERATION or two ago, Maggie would not have been going to school at all. She would have been deemed uneducable. But on a sunny September morning she was included with the other eager first graders. What I saw in that nervous and excited group of young people who were lining up outside the school doors was a subset of our larger community in all its diversity. On this day, as we walked hand-in-hand to join the line, I had a vision of the contributions my daughter will make in her classroom. I think she will be a teacher.

Maggie will teach her classmates about patience. Our culture seems driven by a need for speed. Decisions must be made now, or yesterday, and many people are often frustrated by the snail-like pace of government or the courts, to say nothing of the supermarket check-out line. Maggie sometimes takes a little longer than others to do things, especially when she is first learning new routines and activities. But, with patience and repetition and quiet persistence, she learns everything she needs to know.

Maggie teaches that those who are quick to grasp a new idea may need to take some care to help those who are not so quick. It is important for her classmates and new friends to understand that people are different, and for them to gain this understanding through direct experience with Maggie. Learning to recognize that not everyone sees and experiences the world in the same way and learning to have empathy for different views and ways of behaving is a good thing for them to learn. Maggie will help her classmates develop the quality of compassion.

Another key outcome of Maggie's presence is relationship. Maggie will be unable to attain the same level of individual independence as many of her classmates. She must depend on relationships with other people in order for her to enjoy a good life. This is, in fact, the same for all, regardless of ability or inability. None of us can exist in complete independence. We all depend on others and we cannot exist in complete isolation. Yes, we are individuals and each of us is unique. This is also the case for Maggie. But her presence in the class will teach her community about the necessity and importance of relationships, not just for her, but for all of them and, indeed, for everyone. ∎

step two

Nurturing friendship

There is probably no one who can ever look after your relative with the same persistence, interest, and determination as you do. That's a fact. However, unless you've tapped into the fountain of youth, you won't be around forever. That's a fact, too. So what's the next best thing? The best guarantee of a safe and secure future for a person with a disability is the number of caring and committed friends, family members, acquaintances, and supporters actively involved in their life. It's as simple as that.

> Friends make
> gifts and gifts
> make friends.
>
> INUIT PROVERB

The real strength of these caring relationships comes not just in their connection to the person with a disability but in their connections with each other. Imagine a spider's web. The strands extend from the centre of the web to the edge. Imagine if there was nothing else holding them together. They would flap in the wind. Their functional value would be minimal. They need to be linked with each other in order to form the web, otherwise, the spider would starve. The strength of the web comes when all components are interconnected.

It's the same for our family members. The focus of support for people with disabilities must be placed both on their individual relationships

Worksheet 4 – Relationship circles

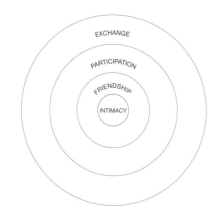

On page 54, we provide instructions to complete your own sample relationship circle.

Make sure that the names of the people you place in the circle of participation are there because of a common interest, hobby, passion, and so on. This will make the chance of people moving into the circle of friendship more likely.

and the relationships among the members of the personal network. These interconnections create the web of support that begins to approximate the thoroughness with which families care for each other. PLAN's specialty is facilitating these caring relationships for people with disabilities. We call them Personal Networks.

A Personal Network is a team. People who come together for three basic purposes: the safety, health, and well-being of your relative, the person at the centre of the network. A healthy Personal Network is one where all members are in touch with each other, coordinating their involvement, and staying on top of things. They are united by bonds of friendship, love, and trust. This is the sum of everything you embody but won't be able to provide forever.

The role of friendship in our lives

The oldest literature from all cultural traditions attests to the importance of friendship. Themes about our interconnectedness are but one indication that we are, above all else, social beings. Friendship is a necessity for all of us, as important and essential to life as food and drink.

Aristotle, a Greek philosopher and major influence on Western thought, put it succinctly: "Without friends no one would choose to live, though he had all other goods." Perhaps it's because friendship is so fundamental to our existence that we take it for granted… or we aren't conscious of its importance until it is brought to our attention.

Lucien Bouchard—a former Canadian political leader—commenting on his recovery from a life-threatening illness underscores this point. Aside from the centrality of his wife and children to his thoughts, he observed that much of his time during recuperation was spent counting the blessings of friendship. In particular, he recalled those friendships that had lapsed or had been fractured and his determination to repair them.

When asked to boil our life down to its basics, most of us would agree that we are *inter*dependent not *in*dependent beings. The impact of this recognition is far greater than our contemporary society appreciates

The healing power of friendship

- People with supportive social ties are less likely to become ill.
- Social contact helps us to heal more quickly.
- Social supports affect the sense of control we have over our well-being and improve our ability to stick with healthy behaviour patterns.

> If you love someone, put their name in a circle, instead of a heart, because hearts can break, but circles go on forever.
>
> AUTHOR UNKNOWN

or acknowledges. Understanding this interdependence is critical to our health, our quality of life, our sense of belonging, our peace of mind, and our security. And, therefore, it is also fundamental to the future security of our family members with disabilities.

The foundation of this future security is not the size of the estate you leave or whether you have a Will. Yes, these are important factors in building a successful Future Plan. But they are not enough. We agree with Emily Dickinson who wrote, "my friends are my estate." Caring relationships and friends provide texture and vitality and makes all living worthwhile.

Friendships—ranging from acquaintances to intimate relationships—are formed by choice. They are freely given, based on mutual interests. Friendships are not one-sided. They are reciprocal, a two-way exchange. They are not paid visitors. They are not volunteers. They are not one-to-one workers.

Good friends support us through good times and bad, when we are on our best behaviour, and when we are not. We don't change ourselves to be with friends. Our gifts and our frailties are accepted as part of who we are. Our friends are not expected to fix us. They are just there. Friendships are naturally enjoyable.

When we are truly loved and valued, we gain a sense of belonging. When we feel like we belong, we change for the better. Our confidence improves as does our self-esteem, our sense of well-being, and our quality of life. Life takes on new meaning. At PLAN, we have consistently witnessed this transformation.

Caring Relationships: a source of support

Think of our own lives. When someone close to us dies, we are not left alone. We still have supportive friends and family. We want this same caring, secure environment for our family member with a disability when we die. This means formalizing the existing relationships of our relative into a Personal Network or creating a new Personal Network around them. It is the only answer to the question, "Who will replace you when you are gone?" Personal Networks can become the next best thing. Personal Networks can become your eyes and ears, arms and legs. Nothing offers peace of mind better than that.

The good feelings that arise from our connectedness to others are an obvious benefit of friendship. However, these good feelings are just the beginning in evaluating the benefits of caring relationships. Investing in an extended network of friends and family for our relative provides both short-term and long-term returns.

When it is time to monitor and advocate, our relatives with disabilities will benefit from the presence of friends and supporters. Individuals who lack supportive ties are vulnerable to a wide variety of negative consequences. If not surrounded by people who have a vested interest in their well-being, our relatives may be at risk for abuse, neglect, and exploitation. Further, the needs of our relatives can be ignored by a busy, overworked service system unless friends are present.

Success in school and on the job is directly correlated with the size and health of our social networks. Social networks are also a

Reciprocity

Personal Network members often describe how meaningful their relationship is with the person at the centre of the network. They talk about getting as much as they give. This is called reciprocity.

A few years back, we commissioned a study to document the experiences of Personal Network members. The results were impressive and confirmed our belief: people with disabilities make a real difference in the lives of Network Members. We also confirmed that the relationships between people with disabilities and Network Members were mutual. In the context of relationships, our family members are contributors.

determinant of health. There is now a mass of evidence to indicate that social ties may be one of the critical factors distinguishing those who remain healthy from those who fall ill. Did you know that the health risks of being isolated are as detrimental as cigarette smoking? Clearly, friendships are necessary for good health.

The power and potential of Personal Networks have far exceeded our expectations. Over the past 20 years, we have seen members of PLAN's Personal Networks:

- monitor the formal programs and services that our relatives receive
- become effective advocates
- serve as executors and trustees or as advisors
- act as supportive decision-makers
- respond promptly and effectively to crises
- solve problems and handle the unexpected
- carry out the wishes of parents.

Stages of a personal network

PLAN hires a Community Connector, who works an average of two to six hours per month, to create and nurture its networks. Vickie Cammack, Founding Director of PLAN Institute for Caring Citizenship, CEO of Tyze, and a co-author of this book, developed this program. She advises that Community Connectors should "do as much as necessary and as little as possible."

Personal Networks take time, sometimes as long as one to two years before they have "legs," as Vickie describes it, or until the network members develop a close and caring relationship with each other and with the person at the centre.

Personal Networks go through three stages:

STAGE ONE: EXPLORATION This is the time for the individual, family, and the Community Connector to get to know each other; it's the time to focus on interests, passions, and possibilities for meeting others. At the end of this period, the Community Connector will provide a set of objectives, a time line of activities, and a list of potential network members.

STAGE TWO: DEVELOPMENT This is the time when all the leads and possibilities are followed up, contacts are made, and invitations extended. The goal in this stage is to recruit network members and to introduce them to each other. Practical strategies are developed.

STAGE THREE: MAINTENANCE By this time, caring relationships have formed and networks meet regularly. The network settles in for the long run. As new interests emerge—and they often do—new connections are made. The network gets stronger and becomes more dynamic.

The art of making friends

Did you know that over 50 per cent of the first attempts that pre-schoolers make to join in a group with other children are rejected? They must keep trying before being accepted by their peers.

In other words, the first step in meeting another person is a learned skill that comes with practice. This is a skill that most of us take for granted and which developed more or less naturally for most of us. A psychologist, Dr. Michael Guralnick, has observed that children with disabilities often do not experience this trial and error process. He suggests that there are three skills which very young children develop while playing with each other:

1. They learn how to initiate contact with peers;
2. They learn how to maintain play. These are the skills we learn to keep the interaction or relationship going;

Qualities of community connectors

PLAN's talented Community Connectors share similar characteristics. They:

- recognize and nurture the capacities and gifts of everyone
- pay attention to detail
- are great event planners

- are creative, pragmatic, and reflective
- know their community and use their connections.

Friends,
by sharing time
with us, are
saying that we
are worth the
gift of time.
I am excited to
be a Community
Connector
because I can be
a part of creating
this opportunity
in someone
else's life.
JOSHUA, A COMMUNITY
CONNECTOR

3. They learn conflict resolution. Inevitably in any caring relationship, we have to learn to negotiate, to share, and to compromise.

Friendships rarely develop by chance. We cultivate them as carefully as we nurture a job or a family, a talent or a hobby. Some of us may think that friendships happen naturally and that, if they don't occur, there is nothing we can do about it. Not true. There appears to be a certain skill set associated with initiating and developing our acquaintances and friendships.

The ability to make friends may have to be relearned for some people. As a result of an accident or injury, their friends may have drifted away and their social circle changed dramatically. They may have had limited opportunity for socializing as a result of institutional living. They may be surrounded by staff that don't recognize the importance of friendship or don't know how to facilitate it. They may have tried to make friends, were rebuffed, and then became discouraged from trying again. They may lack or have lost confidence. They may believe that no one would want to be their friend.

Because friendships do not always develop naturally for some of our family members with disabilities, it is often necessary to approach the development of caring relationships in a focused and strategic manner. It is for this reason that PLAN hires a Community Connector to assist with developing and maintaining its Personal Networks.

What we've learned about personal networks

- They take time, about two years on average, to become a smoothly functioning team.
- It is important to focus on people's interests, passions, and what they *can* do. There are enough people focusing on what they *can't* do.
- Connections among and between network members are as important as their relationship to the person at the centre.
- There are more people interested in developing a caring relationship with your relative than you may think!

How caring relationships challenge families

While many families recognize the importance of caring relationships in their relative's life, they often feel some ambivalence when it comes to actively seeking opportunities for these relationships to form. From our experience, there are three challenges that families face: asking, opening, and believing.

ASKING To ask is to make ourselves vulnerable. There is always the possibility of refusal. Yet reaching out and asking is integral to developing and deepening our relationships. Friendships often form because we ask others to participate in a shared activity. We invite acquaintances over for tea to get to know them better. We ask neighbours to help us with building a fence. We ask friends to give us a hand with setting up for a party. Each of these casual invitations presents an opportunity for the relationship to grow into a caring one.

This process is not as easy when it comes to reaching out on behalf of our family members. We grew up with the unwritten expectation not to complain and to take care of things ourselves. We are fiercely and justifiably proud of our self-sufficiency.

We may feel that extending even a casual invitation is risky. We worry that others will feel obliged—or worse—that they might be saying yes because they feel sorry for us or for our relative. This worry speaks to how deeply many of us have been hurt by negative cultural stereotypes about disability. It makes us forget the gifts our relative has to offer. It makes us forget that others may indeed care.

We need to remind ourselves of the beauty and richness our family member has added to our lives and to the lives of those around them.

> I let go and trusted. We moved fast and wild. I had no idea what it looked like, nor did I care. The dancer inside me was out.
>
> BONNIE SHERR KLEIN

Tyze is an online service that works to create and maintain Personal Networks and is based on the proven PLAN network facilitation model.

Tyze is an alternative to Facebook, assisting to connect, inform, and inspire among network members and with your relative. It is a place to celebrate contributions and achievements; it is a way to stay connected to friends and loved ones. Please visit www.tyze.com.

Nick's network

WITH SUPPORT from his friends, family, and caregivers, as well as his Tyze network, Nick goes to concerts, reads computer magazines, and even has a blog called The Hockey Ambassador. When he found out that some retired NHL players were going to be visiting his home town, he invited them over for a beer and used the Web to special order some Molson Canadian for the occasion. Nick has a vibrant life studying Information and Communication Technologies. Despite being largely bed-ridden with chronic pain, he lives an extraordinarily rich life.

With support, Nick is able to study at the university. His team of friends and caregivers know when his assignments are due and are available to help him write reports and tests. He relies on his caregivers—some of whom only work once in a while—to book transportation to and from concerts, record NHL games, and bring him to hospital appointments.

It's a lot to remember, and a lot to coordinate. And that's where Tyze comes in.

Nick's parents, friends, and caregivers have come to rely on his Tyze network as a critical part of how they manage his care. Nick's parents—along with his live-in caregiver and other agency coordinators and professional caregivers—login to Tyze on a regular basis to see what medications and side effects they need to be aware of, what transportation might be required that week,

and what personal projects Nick has on the go. Donna, Nick's Mom, tells us that they need to run a "faultless system that allows staff to coordinate everything in Nick's life" which is a considerable task, given how busy he is.

Before they started using Tyze, there was a white board in Nick's room with information for the current day as well as the four days prior, but the caregivers just didn't read it. Donna still had to verbally communicate all the critical elements of Nick's day and medical needs to each new caregiver as he or she arrived, and she worried that things would fall through the cracks.

With Tyze, communication is now ongoing and Nick's caregivers have access to the information they need, whenever they need it. Tyze commands their attention in a way that the white board did not, in part because they are young and they understand computer communication, but also because the information is timely and relevant. Every time an entry is made regarding Nick's care and schedule, his caregivers receive an email message. Each caregiver knows that they have to start their shift by logging into Nick's Tyze network to stay current.

Some of the caregivers access Nick's Tyze site using their iPhones, so that they can send and receive messages while they're on-the-go. Passwords, medication information, social activities and doctor's

continued on next page

appointments are all stored within Nick's private, Tyze network so that his team of caregivers can share information and stories, and deliver the best possible care.

Nick is a sports fan, technology enthusiast and indomitable spirit with high hopes for his future. He's curious about the world, and fearless when it comes to using technology. With the support and involvement of his friends, family and caregivers, Tyze is playing a significant role in helping him to achieve his dreams. It provides seamless communication for all the people who have Nick's care as their common objective. ∎

Persistence and patience, one network at a time

If there is something I have learned in my role as facilitator, it is that it takes persistence and patience to develop a network. I remember hearing that usually, people will say yes when asked to be on someone's network. Well, if they don't, what do you do? Ask again in a different way. And if they still say no? Well, then, ask a third time.

I attend social gatherings, observe, and then decide what areas I want to involve myself in. The bottom line is that until someone is actually part of the network, they do not see the benefits.

Being a network member means having a reciprocal relationship with the focus person. Rose, my focus person, keeps me on track with our progress when I get caught up with logistics. For instance, when I start taking out my calendar, she just says, let's ask them next weekend when we see them.

I think it's knowing when to plan and knowing when all the plans in the world don't matter, it just seems the time is right. Start with a few and they will come. I'm faced with challenges and rewards on a weekly basis. That's why this role is so interesting!

BETTY HAHN-SIDOR
PLAN Edmonton Network Coordinator

Seven key elements of a resilient social network

1. reciprocity
2. sustainability
3. hospitality
4. context of participation

5. boundaries
6. letting go
7. relationship to service.

We constantly hear stories from ordinary people attesting to how their relationship with our sons and daughters has brought meaning to their lives. These are often people who wanted to reach out but did not know how. Each invitation we offer is an opportunity for others to extend their community and to broaden their relationships.

OPENING In order for others to come into our lives, there needs to be a place for them. It is impossible to meet people or deepen a friendship if we have no time to spend with them. This is an issue for many people with disabilities. Virtually all areas of their lives may be programmed. From an outsider's perspective, there is no apparent need for a friend. Our relative may be too scheduled for friends and acquaintances to spend time with them. We may need to give up a program or change schedules to create the space that would allow for others to engage with our relative.

On a more subtle level, some of our own actions might inhibit the involvement of others. Over the years we may have become used to doing many things for our family member. The presence of others changes our routines too. The involvement of somebody new might be threatening. Shouldn't we be doing it ourselves? That's good, old fashioned guilt talking. We can do it better. What if they do it better? What will they think of us? That's letting fear do the talking for us. As we feel ourselves losing some control, we may resist or undermine the contributions of others. We need to ask ourselves honestly and courageously what we are willing to let go of in order to make room for others to become active and involved in the lives of our relatives.

When you really think about it, this process of letting go is our lifetime task. It is why you are reading this book. Friendships provide a catalyst to accomplish this task. Our family members grow richer from having experiences outside of their immediate family. Their friends can inspire and encourage them to participate and contribute to society.

BELIEVING   Of the three challenges, this may be the greatest. We worry that the distinctive traits or history of our relatives may make them unlovable—to everyone, that is, but us. We remember the absence of invitations to birthday parties or sleepovers. We notice, yet again, someone staring in the supermarket or when we receive a look of pity from a passer-by. We feel hurt by these things and we ache for our relative. Our overwhelming desire is to protect, and we cannot find it in ourselves to truly believe there is a caring community of people available to befriend our relative. This lack of belief affects our ability to be open to others, and to trust in their integrity.

After more than 20 years of nurturing Personal Networks at PLAN Canada and in dozens of locations around the world, we can assure you that no disability can prevent a caring relationship from forming. No previous experience, no characteristic, no behaviour, not anything. And we don't just believe this, we know it. The proof is in the hundreds of friendships that have developed within our Personal Networks.

In spite of the negative view of an uncaring society profiled regularly in the media, people do reach out to each other. PLAN's experience bears this out. People are genuinely hospitable and eager to become part of our relatives' lives. Often they just need to be asked.

Our challenge as parents and families is to not let our fears dominate the opportunities for friendship.

The heart keeps looking for itself. It knows and does not know where it belongs.

JAN ZWICKY

Relationships and contribution

Relationships play an important role in enabling our sons and daughters to contribute their gifts. From the comfort of supportive friends, family, and Personal Network members, people with disabilities can find opportunities to work, volunteer, create, inspire, care, serve, and contribute.

Our family members make contributions in two ways:

CONTRIBUTIONS OF DOING These are the action-oriented contributions we are most familiar with such as volunteering and working.

CONTRIBUTIONS OF BEING These are contributions made by the majesty of our relative's presence. Being present is an important way for our family members to make their contributions. The exchange is fellowship and communion. Our relatives offer grace, caring, attentiveness, wonder, acceptance, silence, receptivity, compassion, inspiration, pleasure, gratitude, loyalty, and friendship. These gifts—often overlooked in our society—are critical to society's well-being. In fact, they are a necessary antidote to "too much doing."

Identifying the gifts and contributions of our relatives can lead to meaningful relationships. See Worksheet 5 on page 57.

For more on the relationship between contribution and citizenship, visit www.philia.ca.

That's what friends are for

There is something about being human that makes us yearn for the company of others, to be with and to be touched by our family and friends. Isolation and loneliness are devastating by-products of having a disability. We believe that these by-products are disabilities in and of themselves.

Loneliness can weigh even heavier when a person with a disability is served by a large, impersonal service delivery system which has little time or resources to focus on friendships. The only way to truly diminish this loneliness is by paying attention to caring relationships. Even though this may be challenging for both our family member and for us, it is critical for their future security and well-being.

The keys to creating these connections are first, our willingness to let them happen and second, our effort to make them happen. All the riches of the world will not compensate for the security of being cared about. That's what families do. That's what friends are for.

Significant contributions

Personal Network members make significant contributions because they:
- see the gifts and abilities of our relatives
- validate our relatives by letting them know they are valued
- help our relatives develop their talents
- create opportunities for our relatives to make contributions.

Enough talk: the belonging initiative

There has been a lot of talk over the years about the importance of friendship for people with disabilities. Unfortunately there hasn't been a lot of action, until now that is.

A group of Canadian organizations has banded together to do something about ending isolation and loneliness. Members include L'Arche Canada, the Canadian Down Syndrome Society, Canadian Abilities Foundation, Independent Living Canada, Inclusion Press, Developmental Disability Resource Centre, Laidlaw Foundation and, of course, PLAN and the PLAN Institute. For more information, please visit www.nurturingbelonging.ca.

Friendship

Some friendships last for several years.

Friends share the good and bad times together.

Friendship is about helping people by

being there for them when they are in trouble.

Friendship is about helping friends

deal with difficult situations.

Friends should always stay in touch with each other.

Friends should care about others enough

to try to support them in times of crisis.

When you are down, a friend can lift you up.

Some friendships last a lifetime.

JENNY BAKER

Worksheet 4

Relationship circles

For most of us, relationships with family and friends are what keep our lives on track. We have a whole range of relationships–family, partners, lifelong friends, work colleagues, neighbours, people with whom we share an interest, right through to people whom we pay to provide services.

For people with disabilities, these relationships are equally important but can sometimes be challenging to create.

We needn't leave friendships and relationships to chance. We can be really intentional and make it easier for people with disabilities to strengthen their networks. We can do this by enabling them to go to places where they can engage in existing or new interests, hobbies and passions, and have the opportunity to meet people who share these interests.

Use the relationship circles tool on page 56 to look at the people your relative already has in their life. It will help to map out their community as well. It can be completed one-to-one, or with family and friends, or even brought to a network meeting to complete as a group.

In the relationship mapping diagram, the concentric circles are used to plot out relationships. Marsha Forest, Jack Pearpoint and Judith Snow describes these circles as:

- The circle of **intimacy**
- The circle of **friendship**
- The circle of **participation**
- The circle of **exchange**.

CIRCLE 1 The circle of intimacy is concerned with loving relationships and the anchors in your relative's life. In here, go the people your relative cannot imagine life without. Typically Mom, Dad, partner, closest friend, children. Your relative doesn't need to get on with them all the time!

CIRCLE 2 The circle of friendship is concerned with the friends and allies of your relative. Good questions to ask your relative are: Who do you call when you've got good news? Who do you moan to when you've had an argument with your partner/your parent(s)? Who do you draw strength from, share a laugh with, and share your dreams with?

CIRCLE 3 The circle of participation is concerned with shared interests and a neighbourhood connection. In here are people your relative knows from clubs, committees, work, and so on. **NOTE** This circle is particularly important because it is the building block for circles 2 and 1. The more connections made in this circle will increase the likelihood of building meaningful connections in circles 2 and 1.

CIRCLE 4 The circle of exchange is concerned with paid relationships. In this circle are people like your relative's doctor, dentist, window cleaner, hairdresser, taxi driver, and so on.

What will emerge when your relative's diagram is complete is a picture of how your relative's network is or isn't in balance. For example:

• many people with disabilities have the same number as other citizens in Circle 1, but few in Circles 2 and 3 and markedly more in Circle 4

• some people with disabilities spend most of their lives with people who are paid to spend time with them, that is, those in the outer circle, the circle of exchange.

The main strategy for strengthening the inner circles is to bring people in to Circle 3, the circle of participation. These are people who spend time sharing an activity of mutual interest—anything from working together, playing a sport, sharing an art or craft activity, to going out for a meal together or going to the theatre.

Through participation, people become friends over time.

We also know that people don't come straight into Circle 2, the circle of friendship. Friendship doesn't happen instantly.

Relationship Circles

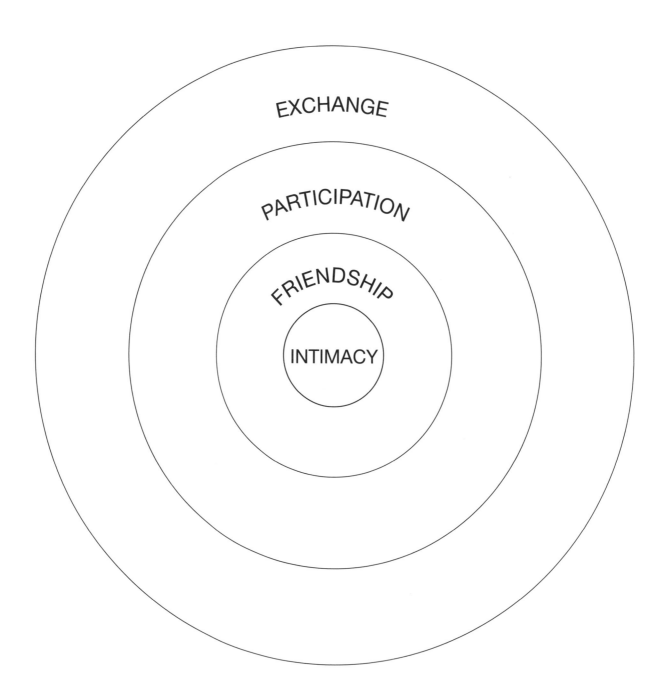

Worksheet 5

Contribution

The following questions may help you identify the various ways your family member makes or could make a contribution.

We suggest you answer these questions and then share with your family member and others who know them well.

What contribution does your relative make to your family?

What are the three activities they love the most?

What are their passions?

What gives them the greatest joy and pleasure?

Who are their heroes?

What famous public personality (singer, actor, athlete) do they like?

What are their gifts of doing?

What are their gifts of being?

What would they like to learn?

What could they teach others?

What have you learned from them?

What positive attributes do others like about them?

What is the greatest accomplishment of their life so far?

What job or volunteer position would best suit their interests and personality?

Worksheet 6

Spirituality

Those who have a religion or spiritual world view may use this worksheet to reflect on the things that make a good spiritual life for their family member with a disability.

Faith communities can provide a starting point for building relationships or networks. Whether we practice spirituality formally or informally, the human spirit always needs to be nurtured.

We hope this worksheet will help put the pieces together to answer the question, "Who will ensure that the beliefs that our family member has developed over the years are continued when we are no longer around?"

Is going to a place of worship important to your family member? _____

How often do they like to go? _____

Do they need support to get there? _____

Where is that place? _____

Who is the main contact person? _____

Name and contact details _____

Is there any other organization connected with their faith that they wish to be a part of?

_____

Do they need support to do this? _____

Who is the main contact person? _____

Name and contact details? _____

Does your relative's spiritual belief system involve any special dietary requirements?

_____

If so, please explain.

_____

_____

Are there daily habits, for example prayer at mealtime, that are important to your relative?

_____

What kind of support is needed to make this happen?

_____

Are there any icons or pictures that should be with your family member, either in their house or carried or worn by them to keep their faith alive? _____

Are there any special days or festivals that should be celebrated? _____

_____

How should this be done? _____

Is there anything else about your relative's spiritual belief system that should be noted?

_____

Is there anything needed to make communication easier at the place of worship?

_____

Is your family member accepted by the other worshippers? _____

_____

Is anything needed to make full participation easier, for example, a loop system, large print books, and so on? _____

Are there any physical barriers that prevent full participation? _____

_____

If you are not around at the time of your relative's death, have you left instructions about the wishes for the type of funeral it should be? _____

_____

creating
a home

On a green island in Ontario
I learned about being human
built a house and found the woman
and we shall be there forever
building a house that is never finished

AL PURDY

Maggie the teacher

The lesson of people first

MAGGIE AT 10 YEARS OLD is in grade 4, sings in the children's choir at church, takes dance lessons with a group of girls her age, goes to birthday parties, and likes to get together with her friends. There is nothing remarkable in this, except Maggie was born with a disability.

We hope that Maggie's community will learn that her disability is only part of who she is. They should learn to accept and understand her differences at the same time as they learn to enjoy her smiles and laughter. It is good if they learn that her disability does not keep her from having friends, from going to Guides, talking swimming lessons, doing gymnastics, or singing in a choir.

Her community will learn that she treasures friendships as much as they do and that, just like them, she enjoys having successes and would rather not experience rejection or failure. If her community learns to see her just as Maggie first and foremost, then perhaps they will be able to see others who are different, for whatever reason, in the same way, and that is, as people first.

Our ultimate vision for Maggie is probably not much different from that of any parent. We want her to have friends, to have an education where she learns as much as she can, does the best se can and where she is part of the community of her peers; we'd like her to have the opportunity to participate in post-secondary education if that is her wish, to end up with a rewarding job, to have a home and good friends; and to have a good life that is rich in experiences and where she makes valued contributions to her community.

Although our primary, day-to-day focus is about the fast-approaching transition to high school, we now must think about Maggie as an adult, growing ever independent and one day, wanting to move away from home. ∎

Creating a home

Ahome of one's own. This is the universal dream, occupying a powerful place in our individual and collective psyche. Home as haven and home as hospitality convey the intangible aspects of home. Home is also a feeling—the feeling you get when at the end of a long day you open your front door and exhale, Ah, I'm home.

In Al Etmanski's book, *A Good Life*, he writes about the essence of home having nothing to do with wood, nails, bricks, and mortar. Rather, it's about sweat and laughter, bruises and tears, stains and cobwebs, flowers and slammed doors, failures and promises, kisses and fingerprints. Home is where we can just be, where we become, where we belong. It's our haven and sanctuary, whether it be owned or rented.

> Only when you discover yourself can you be secure.
>
> DAPHNE ODJIG

The word "home" comes from a Sanskrit root meaning a safe place to lie down; a separation of outside from inside, defined by a threshold. Isn't that the kind of place we want for our friends and family members with disabilities? A place that provides continuity and security? A place that ensures privacy and reflects the personality of those who live there?

Making a house a home

Parents the world over rank a stable and hospitable living environment as a high priority for their sons and daughters. A house, however, doesn't become a home by accident. It requires thoughtfulness and care. It starts by understanding the meaning of home to your relative. What are they used to? How can you recreate that? How do you guarantee that a heap of living will take place there? See Worksheets 7 and 8 at the end of this step to help answer these questions.

Some of our sons and daughters will want to have their own place. They'll want to live on their own or with people they know and like. They'll need very little staff support. Others will need intensive staff support.

The road to independence begins at home

"BALANCED AND STABLE" would nicely describe the first 18 years of Andrew's life. In large measure, this is due to the tightly woven family tapestry that provides strong strands of love and support for Andrew.

"Precarious" would describe the challenging process of Andrew leaving high school and transitioning to adulthood. After much deliberation, Barbara and Robert found an agency that would provide daily supports for Andrew in the family home. Stability resumed.

When Andrew 21, however, his behaviour took a radical turn. He became restless. Barbara and Robert were puzzled, especially when Andrew began pulling pictures off his wall.

The answer came one afternoon with a knock at the door. Barbara opened the front door to greet a neighbour… and Andrew! Unbeknownst to his parents, Andrew got up on his knees, opened the front door, crawled down the steps, and with the determination of an Olympic athlete, dragged himself down the driveway and into the alley, which is where the neighbour found him.

It took a few more escape attempts for Andrew to make his point clear: he wanted to move out. He was ready for a change, and he chose the most visual way he knew of to make his message clear.

When Barbara and Robert realized that Andrew was looking for independence, they had the courage to adjust their thinking and take swift action.

They learned of two fellows around Andrew's age who were looking for a roommate. The timing was perfect and Andrew soon found himself transported into a brand new world, albeit 11 minutes from the family home.

Andrew had a large bedroom. He chose the pictures for his walls. He also chose his bedding, as touch is a very important conduit of sensation for him.

When Andrew moved, his day supports followed. His restlessness ceased and he stopped trying to change his surroundings. He was content. Bearing witness to this, Barbara and Robert were able to move forward as well.

Andrew settled in quickly; for Barbara and Robert, however, the transition took longer. Initially, they felt a sense of guilt; then they felt guilty for not feeling guilty. It took them a while to get used to the spontaneity that their new "empty nest" lifestyle afforded them.

Andrew lived a full life in this environment for 14 years. The next time, it was Barbara and Robert who wanted a change. ∎

continued on page 70

Once this sense of home has been clarified, you can examine the type of tenure and other technical details that best suit your relative, and perhaps your pocket book! For example, at the end of this chapter in Jackie's story, we will describe how the assets in an RDSP can be used to purchase a home.

Home can exist wherever you live and regardless of who owns or manages the building, house, apartment or room. The key to creating a home is to have control over the home environment; to make sure it reflects your family member's personality; to ensure that your family member chooses their own roommates.

One of our past Presidents is very satisfied with the group home her son lives in and we have to say we agree with her. Every time she visits Peter, there is laughter—surely one of the languages of home. Mind you, she is a respected advocate, who is on top of everything. She has briefed and prepared Peter's Personal Network to carry on her vigilance.

Regardless of where our relatives live, we want them to have choice. We want our relatives to live in a place that respects their choices, a place where their personality shines through.

Many of us cannot afford to assist our family members in purchasing their own home. We're still paying down our own mortgages. There are alternatives to private home ownership, however, that will provide long-term stability. Housing cooperatives and land trusts, for example, have many of the advantages of home ownership. So does home sharing; that is, living with others who do not have a disability. If these options are not available or appropriate, we suggest you consider rental.

Rental accommodation—particularly rent to own—can allow people to establish a sense of their own place and to maintain control of their living environment. It may not be for everyone but being a tenant provides your relative with the flexibility to try different living arrangements, particularly when they are starting out and first leave home.

We see no reason why people who live in group homes and who need staff support for their personal care should be denied the benefits of living in a home-like setting. This may not be easy. Not every agency

> If mealtime is a renewable resource, then food is a social lubricant that can keep the machinery of involvement and interaction running between people with and without disabilities.
>
> KAREN MELBERG SCHWIER
> AND
> ERIN SCHWIER STEWART

appreciates the difference between house and home. You may have to search for the right agency. You may have to advocate. You may have to change your relationship with the current service provider.

These options are more feasible now. The promotion of individualized planning and funding, for example, demonstrate a respect for the individual's wishes and a commitment to personalized, customized supports rather than catering to the needs of the group.

Limitations of current housing options

Governments spend millions of dollars every year on housing for people with disabilities. That's a good thing. The challenge for advocates and parents alike is to ensure that control of the home environment doesn't rest exclusively with the agency or service provider. The progressive agencies out there today are responsive and sensitive to making genuine homes out of their group living arrangements. But families still worry. What if there is a change in staff, the home supervisor, or in agency leadership? What will happen if there are funding cutbacks?

It's not that group homes, semi-independent living, and other residential options are wrong. But they do have their limitations. In our conversations and meetings with families, the following concerns about the current residential service system for people with disabilities surface repeatedly:

- there is no control over where their relative lives
- individual needs may be secondary to those of other roommates
- someone else decides who your family member lives with
- the personality of the home is often shaped by the people who work there, not by the people who live there
- some group homes may not welcome the involvement of family and friends
- there is no security of tenure
- families fear the loss of caring and understanding staff and home supervisors, as these types of changes have an immediate impact on their family members.

Home ownership means:

- control over where you live
- stability of tenure
- the opportunity to build up equity
- privacy
- a sense of place
- choice
- ability to offer hospitality
- security
- safety and comfort.

As a result, more and more families are looking for alternatives that provide flexibility, continuity, and greater control.

Control is the key

Control is best exercised by ownership. One alternative is for our family member to own their own home. They can own it directly or it can be owned on their behalf through a trust.

This is becoming an increasingly attractive option to families who want to a secure housing option to complement the other elements of the Personal Future Plan they are developing. They see their relatives living in a place they choose, with people they like, with staff they choose to hire (or fire) for as long as they like… actually, that sounds sterile. They see their family member residing in a good, friendly neighbourhood, within walking distance of stores and other amenities, greeted by neighbours and shopkeepers, living with a best friend, hosting dinner parties, and relaxing in a home designed and decorated to their standards and preferences. Does this sound too good to be true? For inspiration, read the Makishi and Nish family stories and consider the housing examples at the end of this chapter.

Home ownership

Homeowners have status in our society. The pride of ownership is one of our more important cultural values. Home ownership is the fulfillment of a dream even if we have a hefty mortgage and are borrowing money from a financial institution. Home ownership can also be a good investment, and a hedge against inflationary times.

Most of us take it for granted that we will own a home at some point in our lives. Until recently, this has not been the case for people with disabilities. In the past, it was a dream they and their families dared not consider. As our families members become more self-sufficient and as our plans to secure the future become more focused, home ownership for people with disabilities is becoming an option of interest. In fact, it is an option that more parents are exploring, more financial institutions are supporting, and governments are welcoming.

Major home ownership initiatives are underway in Australia, the United Kingdom, and the United States. And more and more examples are being developed all over Canada.

Whether the home is owned directly by your relative, owned jointly with you or others, or owned by their trust, for as long as they like your relative will have a choice in where they live, who they live with, and in the staff they hire. As one mother put it, "Roommates will come and go, support services will change, that's a given. But whether I am around or not, I know that the house—or I should say the home—will be there for my daughter."

Critical components of home ownership

As you might expect, making arrangements for home ownership for your family member can be complicated. The mix between financial and legal matters, health and safety concerns, and social support adds more considerations. It means paying attention to a number of critical components.

FINANCING THE PURCHASE Unless you are independently wealthy, this is a major challenge. The Registered Disability Savings Plan (RDSP) provides families with a means to begin saving for the purchase of a home. The matching Canada Disability Savings Grant, the Disability Savings Bond, and investment income will increase the size of the capital your relative will have available. The details of the RDSP are discussed in Step Five.

Other financing options used by families include:

- re-mortgaging the family home to access additional capital
- forming a partnership with other parents to purchase a home
- taking out a reverse mortgage
- working with local developers who, in return for zoning concessions from municipalities, will make affordable housing available
- earmarking part of their estate to establish a housing trust exclusively for the purpose of purchasing a home

- purchasing life insurance to finance a home or establish a housing trust
- renting out the other bedrooms to help finance mortgage payments.

ASSISTANCE WITH RENOVATION The Canada Mortgage and Housing Corporation (CMHC) under two programs—the Residential Rehabilitation Assistance Program (RRAP) and the RRAP-D Program— offers financial assistance to homeowners and landlords to improve their dwellings so they are more accessible to persons with disabilities. The amount you receive is based on the cost of mandatory repairs and the area in which you live. Currently, the maximum loan amounts range from $16,000 to $24,000. A certain amount of the loan may be forgivable, depending on income. Higher amounts of assistance may be available in more remote areas. For further information, see Resources on page 209 in order to contact CMHC Prairie and Territories Region.

OWNERSHIP Here are some home ownership options you may want to consider for your relative:

- they have direct title
- they co-own the house with another person (for example, their spouse or a family member)
- you own the house together
- at least two families own the home
- your family member lives in a housing co-op that can build up equity
- your family member rents to own
- you arrange financing for your family member to live in a co-housing development. All financing (for each unit and the common areas) comes from the owners of all the units

> The future has already arrived. It's just not evenly distributed yet.
>
> WILLIAM GIBSON

CONTINUED FROM PAGE 64

Andrew becomes a homeowner

WHEN BARBARA came across a new condo development targeting first time home buyers, she knew this option had potential for giving Andrew what his brothers and sister had: the sense of pride, respect, and acceptance that comes with home ownership.

Many hurdles would have to be cleared before this dream could be realized. First, try finding a mortgage lender when the main applicant is on AISH. Thankfully, the mortgage broker understood what Barbara and Robert were trying to achieve (it took going back to CHMC no less than four times to convince them that it was possible for Andrew to become a home owner).

Andrew didn't possess a credit card, something he'd need in order to establish a credit history. Barbara and Robert quickly ordered one up and began using it in order to create a credit history for Andrew.

The mortgage was finally approved, but the celebration was stalled when Barbara and Robert realized that they would have to apply to the Courts to become Andrew's formal trustee with the ability to buy and sell property (see Continuum of decision-making options for adults with disabilities in step 4). Upon reviewing the application, the judge wanted confirmation that Andrew, having only AISH as income, could make the financial commitment. A meeting with Barbara and Robert convinced the judge how home ownership would benefit Andrew — not just for the roof over his head, but also for his standing in the community.

Andrew moved into the condo on a tenant-at-will basis (that is, he received possession of the property prior to paying the full purchase price) while his parents sorted out the trustee issue. Land Titles didn't agree with the wording of the first Trustee Order, so back they went to Court to have it changed.

Andrew's condo has two bedrooms and a den, which is perfect for having both a roommate and support staff. It is a bungalow, which won't present any accessibility issues for him or for his future roommate. It has a back patio and a great welcoming feel to it. It is close to both the family home and a bus route so Andrew can still access regular city transit.

Andrew's agency and staff respect the family's point of view and understand that they are guests in Andrew's home.

continued on page 72

- the house is owned by a trust in your family member's name (or by joint trusts if two or more people with disabilities are involved). The trust(s) can be established:

  - while you are alive; or

  - through your estate after your death.

TYPES OF CO-OWNERSHIP If more than one individual or family owns the home, then you must choose one of these legal co-ownership options:

- joint tenancy; or

- tenancy in common.

HOUSING TYPES Just about anything is possible:

- single family

- condominium or row housing

- housing cooperative unit

- co-housing

- apartment

- mobile home

- infill housing (for example, converting a garage into a small housing unit)

- renovation of an existing house

Joint tenancy

Property owned jointly by two or more persons in which the surviving joint tenant(s) becomes the owner of the entire property when one of the joint tenants dies.

Tenancy in common

Property owned jointly by two or more people. Upon the death of one of the tenants-in-common, ownership of the deceased's shares is transferred to that person's estate, not to the other joint owner.

ANDREW BECOMES...

CONTINUED FROM PAGE 70

The whole family had a good time decorating Andrew's home and were so pleased to see how quickly he settled in. He likes being alone but will eventually need a roommate to help cover expenses.

Being a first time homeowner, Andrew will receive mortgage assistance on a monthly basis for the first nine years of ownership.

Happily, there are many words to describe Andrew's current life: neighbour, home owner, tax payer, secure, happy, involved, respected, host, guest, content, peaceful, busy...

LINDA MCDANIEL

continued on page 76

- purpose-built housing designed for your relative's needs; for example: shared kitchen, dining, and lounge areas.

ONGOING MAINTENANCE If you purchase a house, you will need to make arrangements to cover:

The ongoing mortgage payments

- Will government income assistance be enough?

If not:

- When you are alive, will you supplement the mortgage payments out of a living trust, from family resources or from some other source such as the RDSP?
- After your death, will the payments come out of a trust?

The major maintenance, repair and insurance costs as well as property taxes

- Will you pay for these costs yourself while you are alive or will you establish a living trust for this purpose?
- Will you establish a trust to cover these costs after your death?

NOTE It is critical that you consult with a knowledgeable lawyer to establish the trusts referred to above. For example, you want to ensure that you do not jeopardize your relative's entitlement to government benefits.

Alberta Assured Income for the Severely Handicapped (AISH) allows you to own your own home but has a ceiling on trusts independent of the value of a home held in trust. See Step 5 for more information on trusts.

The minor, ongoing maintenance

While this can be done by yourself in the short term, you may want to consider contracting with a property management company to provide this service. In addition, this may be a service you will need to request your trustee to provide. If your relative lives in a condominium or a housing cooperative, property maintenance is already built into the housing agreement.

Everyone benefits when everyone belongs.

NEGOTIATING FUNDING FOR PROGRAM SUPPORT STAFF Unless you have the private means to pay for staffing supports, you will have to negotiate funding from government. Generally speaking, government is becoming more interested in supporting people to live in their own homes. After all, it represents a big savings if the capital costs of the home are not its responsibility. We suggest you use this argument when negotiating the supports necessary. You can argue that since you are financing the house, the government should finance staff supports.

SELECTING COMPATIBLE SUPPORT STAFF Not every staff person will be comfortable working in your family member's private home. Many staff will see it primarily as their workplace. We suggest you spend time clarifying in writing the values that are important to your relative. When hiring through an agency, become familiar with their operating philosophy. Interview their executive director. Visit some of their programs. Get to meet the people who receive services from them. Talk to their families.

Do not be afraid to let staff go if it appears they are not compatible with the values established for the home.

CHOOSING A COMPATIBLE ROOMMATE There is no scientific approach to this challenge. Some people are easy to get along with. Others are not. Often you won't know until you try. Many of the people who are now living in their own homes first tried living on their own in some form of rental accommodation. Then they invited someone to live with them. This is an excellent way to test the kinds of support you and your relative will need. It also enables people to have a better sense of who they want in a roommate.

TECHNICAL ADVICE FOR CONSTRUCTION AND RENOVATION
We'll leave you to your own devices with this component. You will be able to access building contractors in your area far better than we will. Accessible building design advice is available from local disability resource groups if you would like additional expertise. Other parents are a good connection for families who are considering construction or renovation.

Looking to the future

Times are changing. More people with disabilities are about to become homeowners. They are gaining a measure of choice and control over their lives that they have never experienced before. When established with due respect and consideration for the issues identified here, home ownership also provides families with a concrete component of their plan for the future.

Families see themselves as part of the solution. With tax and trust concessions, more and more families will be willing and able to invest in the housing future of their relatives with disabilities and to partner with government.

This step—Creating a Home—connects with the other steps in this book. It does not exist in isolation. Without the existence of a network of personal support, our relatives will be just as isolated in their own place as anywhere else. Similarly, you will need to use your Will and trust agreement (see Step Five) to formalize the arrangements to own or rent as well as to make provisions for housing maintenance.

In addition, the next step—Making Sound Decisions—provides an overview on supported decision-making. This Step will assist you to protect your relative against exploitation in their home, to support their choices, and to monitor the home arrangements that have been made.

If we only knew then… advice from Barbara and Robert

When we began this process, we had no idea what we were doing! Mortgage approval should have been last on the list but instead we did it first. We realize now that we went about things totally backwards.

Along the way, we have met people and have had experiences that we otherwise would not have had. We have Andrew to thank for that.

We have learned the art of perseverance and cautious optimism and are able to share with others the importance of holding onto the dream and vision they have for their sons and daughters.

We discovered that there are people in our community who "get it" and understand our vision and wholeheartedly celebrate our successes.

We have learned that "I give up and can't do it anymore," is only temporary and doesn't slow us down.

We would do it all again, just in the right order. ■

Barbara and Robert Nish

Examples of housing solutions

Given the complexity of issues and the unique circumstances of each individual and family, the following examples should serve only as illustrations of what is possible.

EXAMPLE ONE
Starting young: Jackie

Background

All Jackie wants to talk about is her last dance class, the time her choir got to go to Montreal, and the sleepover with her classmates at a local aquarium. Grade four is a time of wonder and learning.

Don and Jasvir are more serious. Conversation reflects their concern for her security and continued happiness. "We take our choices for granted. Knowing that Jackie will have enough money to pursue her dreams is important to us," says Jasvir. They see the RDSP as a way of ensuring that she can make personal choices when deciding her future. They want her to be able go where she wants to go, to do what she wants to do, and to make choices that make her happy.

Don and Jasvir have discussed the RDSP and are planning to contribute $150 a month for the next 20 years. Jackie's grandparents also want to help. They've talked about contributing $25,000 to her RDSP at the start.

When Jackie is 39 years old, her RDSP will be an estimated $362,000. If she purchases a life annuity, she will have annual income in excess of $18,000 per year.

Another option is to use a lump sum from the plan to assist their daughter in purchasing her own home. If they withdraw $200,000 as a down payment when Jackie is 39, she can purchase an annuity that will pay approximately $8,000 per year for the rest of her life.

RDSP Summary:

Family taxable income: over $78,130

Annual family contribution: $150 a month ($1,800 a year)

Family contributions from age 9 to 28: $61,000 (including $25,000 from grandparents)

Value of Grant: $45,000

Value of Bond: $10,000

Investments: moderate risk (estimated return 5.5%)

Age to begin receiving from the plan: 39

Approximate value of the RDSP when payments begin (age 39): $362,000

Option A: No home purchase

Annuity payments: approximately $18,000 per year.

Option B: Home purchase at age 39

Withdrawal of $200,000 for down payment

Annuity payments: approximately $8,000 per year.

Patricia, living in an apartment

Background

Patricia is 38 years old and lives on her own. After sharing a rental apartment with a friend for three years, Patricia moved into a housing cooperative where she stayed for two years.

Patricia's grandmother had left her a large sum of money which she had placed in a discretionary trust. John, Patricia's father, is trustee.

When Patricia decided to move out of the housing co-op, she and her dad decided to look for an apartment unit she could own. They found an affordable one-bedroom unit, centrally located near a large shopping centre, and close to major bus routes.

Financing

The apartment unit cost $125,000.

Patricia's dad contributed $12,500 of his own money.

The discretionary trust contributed $97,500 in a no-interest second mortgage.

Patricia took out a first mortgage for $15,000.

Features

- Patricia has title to the apartment.

- Since her dad owns only a tenth of the apartment, Patricia is the principal owner. As homeowner she is eligible for the homeowner's grant. Also since this is her principal residence, the apartment is not subject to capital gains should it ever be sold.

- The fact that Patricia's father owns approximately a tenth of the apartment prevents a dishonest person from persuading Patricia to sell or to order major repairs.

- Should the apartment ever be sold, Patricia's father would get his money back and the amount of the second mortgage would be returned to the discretionary trust.

- The mortgage payments—plus hydro and maintenance costs—are equal to the shelter component of the AISH benefits Patricia receives.

Thomas, staying in the family home

Background

Thomas is a 48-year-old man who currently lives with his parents. They want him to remain in the family home after they die. When that day arrives, the house will be placed in a trust for Thomas's continued use. To support Thomas, the family has arranged to establish two trusts (a residential trust and a family trust).

Financing

The parents' estate plan provides for the home, including furnishings, to be left in a discretionary trust for the primary use and benefit of Thomas. The family calls this the "residential trust." The trust would have a small amount of funds to cover minor repairs.

A separate discretionary financial trust will provide additional assets to cover maintenance

Building a loving community… Makishi style

ON THE SURFACE, this is a story about a special construction project. But it's also a story that exemplifies how a community can be strengthened and become more welcoming and whole when it receives the gifts and talents of all its citizens. And, yes, it's also a love story.

Rod Makishi was born with a good disposition, a wicked sense of humour, and a tireless work ethic. His fondest memories growing up are of spending summers helping his Dad work on cars. This is where Rod's passion for all things mechanical began.

Christel Makishi is a thoughtful and shy person. At a young age, she began taking piano lessons and has spent many happy hours sharing her love of music with family, friends, and those in a local care facility.

Rod and Christel met in Junior High. They were friends until high school ended and work opportunities took them in different directions. They fell out of touch but, thanks to some of Rod's friends, they were reconnected 10 years later.

Christel recalls being attracted to Rod's quirky sense of humour; Rod was intrigued by Christel's quiet disposition. Rod asked Christel out on a date. Christel said yes, but this first date couldn't exactly be termed a success. Christel was so quiet that Rod, half way through the date, finally asked if she wanted to go home. With eyes lowered, Christel softly replied, yes.

Many a man would have been discouraged, but not Rod. He persisted, Christel slowly warmed up, and soon they were a couple. Initially, Christel's Dad wasn't sure what to think about Rod, and Rod's Mom was concerned about the couple becoming "too serious." Meanwhile some friends secretly wondered if they'd ever be as lucky.

Eventually, everyone saw the true love in this relationship. Some 20 years after that first date, Christel and Rod said, "I do."

Christel's family was able to secure a mortgage on a property with a tiny house. Sadly, the house lacked charm: there was no insulation, it constantly needed repairs, and the leaking roof made Rod and Christel's home barely habitable.

Both Rod and Christel received AISH; in addition, both held down jobs. But there was never enough left over to do anything about the mounting home repairs.

Rod and Christel had developed a strong connection with the Lethbridge Association for Community Living (LACL) and the executive director at the time, Tom Cain. Tom gathered a group of 10 volunteers who both raised the money and then fixed the roof. It still sagged but at least it didn't leak anymore.

Tom also connected Rod and Christel with Habitat for Humanity to help with the rest of the repairs. One of Habitat's biggest concerns was whether Rod would be able to fulfill the 500 hours of sweat equity required by recipients. Tom just smiled. What they didn't know was how proficient Rod was with tools... .or how deep his work ethic ran.

By volunteering at a Habitat home already in progress, Rod demonstrated that he was an asset on this and any other construction job Habitat may have for him.

Habitat decided to tear down the original house and start fresh. Soon after, a new foundation was poured and a brand new house securely built on top. The water buckets that dotted the old home like potted plants were packed up and put away. The new insulation would keep Rod and Christel warm for years to come.

Both Rod and Christel are strong community-minded citizens. They believe that if you receive something, you need to give back something. This equilibrium keeps them happy and engaged, and their community strong and inclusive.

In recent years, both Rod and Christel have served on LACL's board of directors. They also give seminars on inclusive education to help teachers understand and see people with disabilities as valued citizens and contributors to society.

Rod and Christel are mentors and role models for those who wonder how far tenacity, commitment, kindness, and love can get you in life.

Linda McDaniel

Post Script

Recently, Rod and Christel received an inheritance. See Step 5, page 164 for details on how setting up an RDSP has helped secure their financial future. ■

of the home, property taxes, extraordinary expenses, and the quality of Thomas's life. The family calls this the "family trust."

Persons with Developmental Disabilities (PDD) will be asked to contribute funding towards the daily support needs of Thomas. For more information, please see Resources on page 210.

Features

• Thomas continues to live in an environment that is most familiar to him.

• Two or more compatible people will live in the home with Thomas and provide a caring and harmonious living environment. In return, they will live rent free and enjoy the home as is customary under traditional rental contracts.

• Should it become necessary to sell the home, the Will contains a provision that the trustees can do so and use the funds from this transaction to acquire an equivalent home for Thomas's benefit. Any surplus funds will be placed in the family trust.

• As the trust owns the property, it will most likely not qualify for the homeowner's grant or supplement.

EXAMPLE FOUR
Surinder, living in a condominium near the family home

Background

Gopal and Dal purchased a two-bedroom condominium for their 28-year-old son, Surinder. The complex is located within three blocks of the family home.

Financing

Total cost of condominium: $170,000.

Down payment from the parents: $140,000.

Surinder's monthly mortgage payments are approximately $300 over a 20-year period.

Features

• Ownership of the home is between the parents and Surinder. As financial protection, Surinder granted his parents a Continuing Power of Attorney for Property.

• Upon the parents' death, complete ownership of the home goes to Surinder. Surinder's sister and her husband will have Continuing Power of Attorney over Surinder's property.

• One of the bedrooms will be rented to a roommate for Surinder.

• A team comprised of a representative of the family, the service delivery organization, and the family of Surinder's roommate will oversee the maintenance and operation of the condominium.

The making of a sanctuary

FOR ONE GLORIOUS SUMMER in the 70's, an old tamarisk tree with wide branches sweeping down to the sand of a Greek beach was my home. Its branches opened like welcoming arms to form my front door. When friends came to call they knew I was home if they saw my sandals carefully set to one side. Inside there was a special crook in one branch that held my cup and toothbrush and plenty of twigs to drape my scarves on. My tree gentled the sun's rays by day and let the stars peek through at night. I felt safe and sheltered by this kind tree. My tree space felt lived in, by me, by others before me and of course by various wildlife who shared it with me. It was definitely the place that felt the most like home during that sun-kissed summer.

One of our treasured family stories is the account of my mother, who upon reading a letter containing my starry eyed account of my life in Greece, burst into tears and wailed, "She's living in a tree. A tree!" For her, my breezy home was not and never would be a home.

That's the thing about a home. It is a very personal feeling. Not so much a place as a space. It is a space that breathes and nourishes us. A space becomes a home when it opens to us as we are, and when we, in turn, get worn into it. Creating this kind of home space when a person is vulnerable or isolated is complex. As families we are often caught in the paradoxical challenge of finding spaces that both open doors and secure locks. This is why cultivating and consulting caring connections beyond us is so important for our relatives. Standing together, we can peek out, open the curtains of our own comfort zones and imagine the living, breathing spaces our relatives can grow their way into.

And out of.

Just as no tree lives for forever, no home, no matter how well planned, financed and built, is ever permanent. True durability lies in the long arms of others who will care for our relatives beyond our lifetime. It is an embrace that will nourish and honour the spirit of our relatives wherever they may live. ■

Vickie Cammack

Life Is ...

Life is not easy but it can be

Life is a miracle

We get down sometimes but we do not stay there

When we are up we lift others with us

It really helps to have faith

Life is full of challenges and surprises

There are lots of joyous and precious moments

It is freedom to do certain things with

your family and friends

It is about making mistakes

It is full of risks

Sometimes we are sad but sometimes

we are glad to know that we are alive and

can feel whether we are sad or glad

So I decided to turn around and be happy

instead of sad

When I look at the sun,

I remember life has begun with light

JENNY BAKER

Worksheet 7

Welcome mat

These are questions you can discuss with your relative. Have some fun and use a variety of props to facilitate your discussion: perhaps have your relative draw a few pictures or make a collage of cutouts from magazines.

What kind of home would you like to live in?_____

_____

Would you like to live by yourself or with other people?_____

_____

Who would you like to help you live in your own home?_____

_____

What would this person help you with?_____

_____

Where do you want to live?_____

_____

Why do you want to live there?_____

_____

What do you want to live close to? (a park, church, recreation centre, bus route, shops, and so on.) _____

What is your favourite room?_____

_____

Do you have a favourite chair? Would you like to have one? Which room would you place it in?

_____

Where would you place your favourite things?_____

_____

What kind of furniture will you need for your own place?_____

_____

What furniture from your family home would you like to have in your own home?_____

_____

Would you keep a pet? What kind?_____

_____

Would you like a garden?_____

_____

Do you like to cook? If so, would you like to have a big kitchen?_____

_____

Would you like to have a quiet room?_____

_____

Which room would you like to have music in?_____

_____

Do you like doing dishes?_____

_____

Do you like to clean the house?_____

_____

Do you like to mow the lawn?_____

_____

How would you decorate:

Your living room? _____

_____

Your bedroom? _____

_____

Your entrance? _____

_____

What colour would you paint the outside of your house?_____

_____

How would you welcome visitors to your home?_____

_____

When you came home at the end of the day, what would be the first thing you would do?

_____

Worksheet 8

When is a house a home?

Here are some simple guidelines and questions to help you evaluate the home-like quality of residential services.

Whose house is it?

Are the individuals who live in the house the ones to determine its structure and tone or is the house geared to suit the staff hired to provide service? For example, are there pictures and other personal mementos scattered throughout the house or are these personal items restricted to the individual's bedroom? Do the staff use their computers in the home as if they were working in an office?

Use your home and your own life as yardsticks for comparison. Do not accept, "well, it's better than where they were." Instead, ask yourself, "Is it as good as I have now?" and "Is it as good as I would want for myself?"

Look around

Are there locks where they are not needed; that is, on the refrigerator, on the clothes closets, and so on?

Are there no locks where they are needed; that is, on bathroom doors, bedroom doors, filing cabinets, medicine cabinets, and so on?

Do people have the same amount and variety of possessions and personal articles as other people their age?

What does it feel like?

Are the rooms comfortable? How about the couch? The chairs? Could you relax here? Does the place feel like a home?

Take a moment to listen

Can you go somewhere for a little peace and quiet? Are there conversations among the people who live here?

Smell

Do you get a scent of home made dinner on the stove or dessert in the oven, or do you smell institutional cleaners and odors?

Taste

Would you enjoy the food that is served or would you merely tolerate it?

Ask

What are the rules? Are they excessive or overly restrictive? Do they make sense to you? Who makes the rules?

Infer

Do the people who live here experience a home with some added support, programming, and needed supervision? Or do they experience an institutional program with a few home-like qualities?

Analyze

What compromises have been made in the name of budget limitations, programming practices, staff needs, and so on? In what ways do these compromises detract from a home-like atmosphere?

Ask yourself

If an opening came up tomorrow, would I ask to move in?

making
sound
decisions

Compassion is maturity
and maturity is acceptance.
Maturity is precisely
the acceptance of yourself
with your own flaws,
as well as others
with their flaws.

JEAN VANIER

Maggie the teacher

The lesson of presence

MAGGIE WILL ALSO teach the necessity for gentleness. Her difficulties in learning and the slower pace of her development mean that she is not as vigorous or as assertive in making her own voice heard. Her responses are slower and she requires time. The expectation that she will be able to move or think as quickly as others is not a fair expectation. She must, therefore, be treated, taught, and dealt with in gentle ways.

She does, however, have contributions to make. She has her own ideas and her own sense of humour. Her experiences and her existence are as valid as any other person's. But in order for her to be heard, she must be treated gently. Gentleness is generally not valued in our culture which, instead, tends to reward competitiveness. But while competition can bring out the best, it can also generate conflict and division between winners and losers. I think the gentleness that Maggie teaches is a good virtue for everyone to learn.

I think Maggie will teach important lessons about respect and acceptance. Her presence shows that diversity is important and good and that it is to be accepted and valued. It enables her fellow students and friends to learn that she is as much a part of their community as is anyone else, regardless of her individual limitations.

She has her own contribution to make in her own way. Yes, her contribution may be different than the contribution of many others. But her presence gives them an opportunity to learn to accept what she brings, regardless of her differences. Indeed, it may help her classmates and friends to respect everyone's uniqueness and to learn the necessity for accepting diversity. Her presence will teach her classmates that difference is important and that difference is to be respected, accepted, and perhaps even cherished.

Perhaps one of the most important things that Maggie will bring to her community is a concrete example of diversity. Her presence enables people to experience something of the diversity that is one of the dominating characteristics of our world. People are not all the same. Yes, we are all human beings, but we are all unique too. It is important that people learn that not everyone is exactly the same as they are or experiences life in the same way they do. It is important for each person's own sense of uniqueness and individuality. It is also important for them to learn to accept and appreciate the diversity of others and of the world. Maggie's presence teaches that diversity encompasses a range, a breadth, that without her presence they might not otherwise learn. ■

Making sound decisions

When you get right down to it, worrying about the safety and security of our relatives is a paradox. On the one hand, we want to protect them from discrimination, exploitation, abuse, neglect, and injury. On the other hand, we want them to have a good life: a life where they enjoy themselves; where they get to try new things; a life where their choices are respected. We want to teach our relatives how to survive and work through adversity. We want them to learn from their mistakes, as all of us must. We want people to recognize their ability to make decisions and to support them to make sound decisions. This type of self-determination makes a life worth living.

> Do not see me
> as your client.
> I am your
> fellow citizen.
> See me as your
> neighbour.
> Help me learn
> what I want
> to know.
>
> NORMAN KUNC

When our children are young, we make the important decisions on their behalf. When they reach the often complex and challenging time of adolescence, however, it's necessary to starting thinking about meaningful ways to include them in the decisions that will impact their lives. Being aware of—and implementing—sound decision-making practices now will create an important strand to your relative's safety net as they make the transition from childhood to adulthood.

It's a delicate balancing act faced by families the world over: keeping our relatives safe while at the same time respecting their choices. Make no mistake about it. This balancing act is a tough challenge. Families find it difficult. So do service providers. So do government and its institutions.

In this step, we guide you through the ways in which you and your relative can create your own balance between safety and choice. We introduce the concept of supported decision-making. We also describe the types of powers of attorney available to you.

Choosing a guardian

For information on choosing a guardian for your minor children, see Choosing a guardian for children under the age of 18 on page 110.

It starts with choice

Choice is like a muscle: if not exercised, it will atrophy.

A good life supports and respects the choices of our relatives. This means recognizing their tastes, preferences, and values; it also means acknowledging our relative's ability to discriminate, to select, and to choose. We know how determined our relatives can be to express their approval or disapproval. We know they often are aware of their limitations and exercise prudent judgment in the face of it. We know they have views and opinions on a variety of topics. Unfortunately, not everyone is aware, understands, or accepts the capability of our family member.

The assumption of others that our family members don't have opinions or cannot make decisions is an additional hindrance. This can lead to ignoring their wishes and eventually making all decisions, big and small, on their behalf.

We want the people involved with our relative to see what we see: a person capable of making their intentions known. We want the people in their lives to be patient, to be willing to listen, and to watch, and if necessary to be willing to learn our relative's unique and perhaps non-verbal communication style. We know all behaviour is a form of communication and we want our relatives surrounded by people who will take the time to search for that meaning.

We are wary of people who won't make an effort to learn how our relatives express themselves, who are too busy, or who ignore—and perhaps worse—think they know what is best for our relative.

Once there is recognition of their choice-making ability, we can turn our attention to supporting our relative to make decisions. This may mean, in certain circumstances, speaking or making decisions on their behalf. We do this informally when we set up a joint bank account or when we accompany them to a medical appointment.

We believe in nurturing the decision-making ability of our relative rather than giving someone else the power to make decisions on their behalf. The decision-making ability of our relative can be nurtured by:

- respecting their inherent decision-making ability
- enabling their own, authentic decision-making voice
- presenting them with genuine choices

- helping them to sort out and understand the options
- supporting them in making the actual decision.

Is offering
choice too
risky?

How big a
risk are you
prepared to
take?

Can you
balance safety
with choice?

Whom do you
trust?

In reality, many people with disabilities are offered few choices in their lives, which can lead to them becoming passive and submissive. By contrast, when we surround them with people who respect their capacity to make decisions, we also create the conditions for our relative to become a self-advocate. This reduces the risk of exploitation, neglect, and abuse. Ultimately our relatives are safer when they are able to speak for themselves.

Take Tim's situation, for example. When we first met Tim his caregivers made all his decisions. They decided what he should wear, what he should do during the day, what time he should have dinner, and so on. These decisions were based on what suited his caregiver's schedule. Tim was never consulted. For example, Tim loved country music but his caregivers didn't, so he never had the opportunity to listen to the country music station.

Over time, Tim retreated so far into the background of his own life that he might as well have been invisible.

Fortunately, Tim and his family joined PLAN. As his Personal Network developed, so did the relationship between Tim and his staff. Eventually new caregivers were hired based on their willingness to learn Tim's communication style.

Change is a constant. It is hard to predict what we, or our relatives, will have to adjust to, and what critical decisions will have to be made in the future. We can make educated guesses about some of the areas we want protected for our relative but there are no guarantees. Rather than wasting our energy on trying to control the uncontrollable, we suggest you prepare for any eventuality by providing your relative with the best possible people to assist them in making their own decisions.

The secret of good decision-making

Have you ever made a bad decision or a decision you regretted? Have you ever changed your mind?

You are not alone. Some of the poor decisions we have made are minor, some alas, are major and we would like to have made different

Supported decision-making for our relative means:

- they actively participate

- their views are sought and taken into consideration

- they are surrounded by caring, knowledgeable, trustworthy people who can assist with their decision-making and communicate their decisions

- their needs are the primary consideration, not the needs of staff or the service system

- the focus is on their abilities and wishes

- all their choices and options are considered

- their tastes, preferences, motives, and ability to discriminate are taken seriously

- their risks, failures, and mistakes are recognized as learning opportunities.

choices. The same is true and will be true for our sons and daughters, all of them, including those with disabilities.

Decision-making means taking risks, understanding consequences, learning from mistakes, and trying again. An old Chinese proverb says the risk is not in falling off the horse, but in lying there.

Relationships are the foundation of sound decision-making

By now it should come as no surprise that relationships and Personal Networks have additional benefits—they enable good decision-making and assist to protect and keep your relative safe.

The first order of business, therefore, is to consolidate your relative's friends and supporters into a Personal Network. Members of a network can monitor the services and programs your relative receives; they can also advocate in order to ensure the quality of those services and programs.

Network members are often more than willing to support good financial, health, and personal care decision-making for your relative.

Supported decision-making

Most of us make decisions by getting advice from others. We face a dilemma, look at the options, gather information, talk to people, and ask for support.

We suggest you formalize this natural approach to making decisions for your relative. Some provinces, for example British Columbia, legally recognize supported decision-making. They are called Representation Agreements in BC. In the absence of a legally recognized supported decision-making agreement, families can assist their relative to create their own supported decision-making agreement that has practical benefit and moral authority.

To ensure good decision-making for your relative with a disability, we suggest you make the concept of supported decision-making the basis of your approach.

1. Do everything you can to enhance and validate the role of family, friends, and supporters as advocates and advisors to the decisions your son or daughter makes. This is a critical role of the Personal Networks of support. Contact your local PLAN affiliate such as LACL, PLAN Edmonton, or PLAN Calgary.

2. Identify and use the existing advocacy system for people with disabilities.

3. Identify people who would be willing to serve as temporary substitute decision-makers.

4. If you must use the legal system, consider a guardian for personal decisions or a trustee for financial decisions for a specific reason and on a time-limited basis, and remember to do so in a way that will minimize the restriction to your relative's freedom to make their own decisions.

There is no magic to the task of keeping people safe and respecting their choices. It is a matter of mastering the high wire. Leaning towards over-protection creates a barren lifestyle. However, leaning towards complete autonomy without supports or safeguards is a license for exploitation. The risk in either direction can be minimized when friends and family are there to provide support.

Progress always starts with bold ideas.

JANE JACOBS

Guiding principles under the new Adult Guardianship and Trusteeship Act

Since 1978, the legislation which has governed guardianship and trusteeship in Alberta was called the *Dependent Adults Act* (DAA).

The DAA was both inflexible and restrictive, in that it did not provide for any legal mechanisms for decision-making options other than a Dependent Adult Order.

Fortunately, Alberta has recently completed a comprehensive review and revamping of the DAA. In October of 2009, the DAA was repealed and the new *Adult Guardianship and Trusteeship Act* (AGTA) came into force. It is based on four guiding principles:

1. An adult is presumed to have the capacity to make decisions until the contrary is determined.

2. The ability to communicate verbally is not the only determination of capacity. An adult is entitled to communicate by any means that enables them to be understood.

3. If an adult requires assistance to make decisions, that adult's autonomy must be preserved by ensuring that the least intrusive form of assisted or substituted decision-making is provided.

4. In determining whether a decision is in the best interests of an adult, consideration must be given to the known wishes, values, and beliefs expressed or held by the adult while the adult had capacity.

The AGTA clarifies and standardizes the issues surrounding capacity assessments by avoiding the "all or nothing" approach to mental capacity. It also provides for a range of supportive and substitute decision-making options which address the reality that all adults have different levels of decision-making abilities.

Continuum of decision-making options for adults with disabilities

From least to most intrusive, the new continuum of decision-making options in the AGTA includes:

Supported decision-making authorizations: allow an adult with capacity to designate a supporter to help them make decisions in

> A good life includes honouring the choices of our relative.

personal matters. These authorizations will allow the supporter to access personal and health information to assist the adult in making the decision.

Co-Decision-Making Orders for personal matters: is a Court Order which may be utilized where the adult is assessed as having a significant impairment; for example, a mild to moderate cognitive impairment but can still make decisions with assistance. The terms of a Co-Decision-Making Order must be agreed to by both the adult and the Court and, once granted, will specify those personal decisions which the adult is required to make in conjunction with the designated co-decision-maker.

Specific decision-making: allows designated health care providers (a physician, nurse practitioner, or dentist for dental care only), to select a relative to make a one-time decision on behalf of an adult who requires a time sensitive decision relative to health care.

Temporary Guardianship and/or Trusteeship Orders: provides for the appointment of a temporary guardian or trustee to make decisions on behalf of an adult in those situations where an adult is believed to lack capacity and is in imminent danger of death, serious harm, or financial loss.

Guardianship and Trusteeship Orders: while these options remain available for adults assessed as incapable, the capacity assessment application process now:

- mandates improved screening and information provisions for prospective guardians and trustees to ensure that the adult's views are included in a report to the Court, if possible, and

- requires that the Court must consider whether any of the less intrusive options could meet the adult's needs.

When should I consider legal guardianship?

Our society has created legal mechanisms to allow another person to take over some or all of the affairs and decision-making of an adult who has been judged "incapable" by Court Order. The person who is determined to be incapable is then referred to as a "represented adult;" the person who takes over the represented adult's personal decisions is

Build a network and they will come

MY NAME IS Christian Bayus and I am 20 years old. I live in St. Albert, Alberta. I live in a newly renovated basement suite below my parents. I love to have friends over to hangout, play games, and watch TV.

This past summer, I got a dog named Marley. I am learning how to take him for walks and have him follow my commands.

I have been a Lifetime Member of PLAN Edmonton for almost two years. My network of family and friends has quickly expanded to 41 members, and it's still growing. I started my network when I was still in high school and that is why it is so big.

With so many members in my Network, I put out a monthly newsletter to keep everyone up-to-date with what I'm currently doing and what I want to do in the future.

Now that I'm finished school, I work as a businessman for Remax two times a week. I love my job because I work with a team. I also work in the Steilow office one day a week. I also help out at my old junior high school—RS Fowler. I help get lunch ready a couple days a week. I am also looking for another job to keep me busy the other days of the week.

Because I also like helping others whenever I have a chance, I volunteer at the Sturgeon Hospital Gift Shop. This job is fun because I get to be the boss of the money. I ring in sales and give change. I also know how to use the debit machine. I just got a pin for working 100 hours.

I love sports of all kinds, especially the Edmonton Oilers. If I have spare time, I love to go to all types of sporting events. I also go bowling, watch movies, or go to plays, listen to music on my iPod, and keep in touch with my friends on Facebook.

In the future, I would like to move out, go on trips, and get married. ∎

CHRISTIAN BAYUS

referred to as the "guardian;" the person who take over the represented adult's financial affairs is referred to as the "trustee;"

We have always had reservations about full Guardianship/Trusteeship Orders:

1. Most Guardianship/Trusteeship Orders were blunt instruments. Even though adults may only need help in certain areas of decision-making, Guardianship/Trusteeship Orders were:

- not easily tailored
- generally obtained on an "all or nothing" basis, and
- resulted in all of a person's personal and financial decision-making powers being removed.

In the end result, the adult could no longer assist with the decision-making process as, in the eyes of the law, they were no longer a "capable" person.

2. Obtaining and thereafter maintaining a Guardianship/Trusteeship Order can be costly, intrusive, and time-consuming.

3. Guardianship/Trusteeship Orders did not allow for joint or supported decision-making; the represented adult had virtually no say in their own affairs.

4. People with intellectual impairments or difficulties in communicating their desires and other noticeable differences were usually presumed to be incapable, which made it even tougher for them to adequately assert their capabilities.

Few people with disabilities will ever need a full Guardianship or Trusteeship Order. In the past, some parents applied to the Courts to become guardian or trustee of their adult son or daughter assuming this would give them enhanced status when dealing with government or service providers. Unfortunately, many parents soon discovered that this process proved to be both frustrating and costly and, in many cases, failed to adequately address the specific needs of their adult children.

Types of decision-making

As you've no doubt learned by now, we strongly advocate that whenever and wherever possible, your relative participate meaningfully in the decisions that affect their own lives. How your relative participates will vary from family to family. One thing is clear: your relative can't participate if they are not involved in the process.

There are situations, however, where it is in the best interest of your relative, your family, and your friends to create a more formal, legally recognized-decision-making tool.

There are two broad areas of decision-making that affect your relative's life:

1. Financial decisions

2. Personal decisions.

Personal Networks are critical to both. Combined with a number of non-legal options, they offer further assurance that decisions will be made that protect and enhance the quality of life of your relative.

1. FINANCIAL DECISIONS There are a number of legal and non-legal options to protect the financial assets of your relative, prevent exploitation, negligence, or impulsive purchases, and to ensure good financial decision-making.

First, an Enduring Power of Attorney may be useful. An Enduring Power of Attorney is a written document that allows a person to confer authority to someone else to make financial decisions on their behalf. When you confer this authority on someone else you don't lose your own authority. The Enduring Power of Attorney can be revoked at any time by the person who conferred it, as long as that person has the capacity to do so. In order to enact an Enduring Power of Attorney, however, your adult relative must be capable of first understanding and appreciating the nature and extent of their financial affairs, which your adult relative may not be able to do. Remember, capacity is not an all or nothing proposition.

Trusts are another option used by families to protect the financial assets of their relatives and to ensure the funds are used in their best interest. Step Five explores this option in more detail. Trustees can be appointed at any time to manage trust funds.

Because the heart is bigger than trouble. And the heart is bigger than doubt. But the heart sometimes needs a little help to figure things out.

CONNIE KALDOR

For many people with disabilities, the only disposable income they have comes from their monthly government allowance, their AISH benefits. As such, the risk of exploitation or mismanagement is lower. Further, the costs involved in obtaining and maintaining a formal Trusteeship Order for the sole purpose of administering the AISH benefits on behalf of your relative is difficult to justify as a reasonable expense. Accordingly, and in recognition of this reality, informal trusteeship arrangements have evolved in Alberta.

Under an informal trusteeship arrangement, monthly AISH benefits are issued by way of a joint cheque made payable to a family member and their relative with a disability. The AISH benefits can then be deposited into a joint bank account which has been established for that specific purpose. Your relative's monthly expenses can be paid from that joint account with minimal inconvenience.

Other practical approaches used by families to safeguard their family member's assets include:

- establishing a joint bank account with their son or daughter
- purchasing property such as a home in joint names.

2. PERSONAL DECISION-MAKING You can divide this category into health/medical decisions and personal care decisions.

(A) HEALTH/MEDICAL DECISION-MAKING

Most families are concerned with whether their relative will receive medical treatment in the event of an emergency, especially if the doctors are unable to obtain legal consent. You need not worry. Doctors and hospitals in Alberta can—and do—provide emergency medical treatment on an emergency basis without consent.

For non-emergency health care, the experience is more varied. Many adults with disabilities enjoy a long-standing relationship with their family doctor. They know each other's abilities and communication styles. In these situations, the capacity of the person with the disability to give consent may not be an issue. The physician is willing to take the time to give the individual the opportunity to express their wishes.

In other situations, it has become common practice for the doctor or other health care provider to consult with parents or other close relatives around health care treatment for the adult with a disability. Health care professionals have long recognized relationships of trust and caring.

A Personal Directive might be considered if your relative has the capacity to grant one. Discuss this option with your health care provider. This legal document allows an adult person (a "donor") to name one or more persons to assist them with health care, nutrition, shelter, clothing, and other non-financial, personal matters/decisions.

A Personal Directive only becomes effective when it is determined that the donor lacks capacity with respect to the specific personal matter at issue. A Personal Directive can also be amended or revoked by the donor at any time, so long as the donor has the legal capacity to do so.

In order to grant, amend, or revoke a Personal Directive, the donor must first have the capacity or competence to do so. This means that the donor must have the ability to understand the relevant information related to the personal decision and to appreciate the possible consequences of that decision.

As mentioned earlier, capacity is not an all or nothing proposition. It is quite possible for your relative to have the legal capacity required to grant either an all-encompassing or a limited Personal Directive, even though they may not be legally competent in other areas. We suggest that you make a point of discussing this with your relative's health care providers.

However, notwithstanding the above, some health care professionals will provide major health care only if the adult with a disability has a Court-appointed guardian. In these situations, the adult's ability to consent is challenged and informal status for family members is not recognized. As a result, families have had to apply to the Courts to become legal guardians of their relative in order to give consent to an operation or health care procedure.

(B) PERSONAL CARE DECISIONS

This is an area of decision-making that is by far the most elusive because the forces are largely out of our control. Our relatives will likely

We become what we behold. We shape our tools and then tools shape us.

MARSHALL MCLUHAN

be dealing with paid caregivers or service providers and educators for the rest of their lives. These service providers will make daily decisions which will have a significant impact on our relative.

We can't predict the future of government funding for these critical supports and the repercussions on the quality of programs and services. We are pleased that regulations and policy set standards for service providers. And we acknowledge the value of accreditation and formal evaluation. But we know this doesn't go far enough. These tend to focus on broad system standards. They don't address the personal daily circumstances of each of our relatives. You might want to consider a Supported Decision-Making Authorization, a Co-Decision Making Authorization, or a Personal Directive as a more formal way to support your relative.

Monitoring and advocacy are natural extensions of our parenting skills.

Summary of legal options

Enduring Power of Attorney: covers financial matters, but not health and personal care decisions.

Personal Directive: covers health and personal care decisions but not financial matters.

Supported Decision-Making Authorization: permits the designation of a supporter to help make personal decisions

Co-Decision-Making Order: formal Court Order which specifies personal decisions which an adult is required to make in conjunction with a designated co-decision maker.

Specific Decision Maker: person designated by a health care provider to make a one-time decision on behalf of an adult who requires a time sensitive decision relative to health care (where no Personal Directive or Guardianship Order exists).

Substitute Decision-Maker: used to seek permission for health care when a Personal Directive or Guardianship Order does not exist.

Temporary Guardianship and/or Trusteeship Order: a temporary Court Order appointing a person to make decisions on behalf of an incapacitated adult who is in imminent danger of death, serious harm, or financial loss.

Guardianship and/or Trusteeship Order: a formal Court Order granting authority to make guardianship (health and personal) decisions and/or trusteeship (financial) decisions on behalf of another person.

While we are alive, we can engage with service providers. We know how important it is to maintain a relationship with them. We have a good idea of how much work this requires and how much time it takes. If there is a concern we can do something about it. We can join an agency's Boards of Directors. We can create our own society. As in other areas of decision-making, Personal Networks are essential. Here are additional options and resources for you to consider.

Family managed supports

Family managed services allow families to hire paid supports for their relative using government provided and approved funds. The family is responsible for hiring, directing, supervising and paying the PDD-funded support people hired to assist their family member. This funding option is available to adults that are eligible for the Persons with Developmental Disabilities (PDD) program.

As part of the assessment, families receiving child-focused services are required to complete an Individualized Family Support Plan (IFSP). The Family Supports for Children with Disabilities (FSCD) worker and the family work together to complete the IFSP. Once the goals have been chosen and the most appropriate services have been determined and approved through FSCD, families may receive those services through a variety of arrangements.

There are two primary considerations: firstly, determining which service providers are available in the region, and secondly, what works best for the family.

Advocacy

Yeats, the Irish poet, observed: "things fall apart; the centre cannot hold." Human services are human creations and are, therefore, by definition, imperfect. Things can fall apart.

Families know this instinctively. The work at PLAN bears this out. We are often called to support an individual, family, or Personal Network as they advocate for change and improvement in a program or service. People who know our relatives make the best advocates. They may not know all the details of service provision and funding, but they are grounded in what is best for our relative and will fight on their behalf. There are many groups in Alberta who offer advocacy and support. For contact information, see Resources on page 203.

An effective personal advocate is someone who:

- cares about our relative
- knows their requirements
- has good problem solving and negotiating skills
- is free of conflict of interest
- is self-confident and willing to be assertive if necessary
- is willing to seek out—and follow—good advice.

We have discovered that Personal Networks are a great training ground for advocates. Parents can impart their skill and wisdom and teach by doing.

Lastly, we should point out the value of teaching our relative self-advocacy skills. They will learn about their rights and responsibilities; how to speak up for themselves; how to support other self-advocates; and gain confidence. There are excellent written resources and many organizational supports in Alberta. For more information, see Resources, page 203.

Who would be there?

WHEN I WROTE this fictional meditation, I had not yet read Jean-Dominique Bauby's extraordinary book *The Diving-Bell and the Butterfly* (see Resources, page 204). His story is better known now as a result of the movie of the same name. At the age of 45, French journalist Bauby suffered a massive stroke that left him without speech and movement. He was, as he says, "like a mind in a jar." Patiently, letter by letter, Bauby tells his story, using one eyelid to signal at what point in the chorus line of letters his friend is to stop transcribing. Bauby's reality is bright, vivid, and compelling.

What would you do in a similar situation?

You are heading to the grocery store on a sunny Saturday morning. You are a careful driver but your mind is elsewhere—on automatic pilot. Suddenly an approaching car jumps lanes and heads towards you. In a terrifying instant your life changes. After the impact you lose consciousness.

You wake up in the hospital. The pain is excruciating. You are unable to move your arms and legs. Then you discover you can't speak. A doctor and a nurse are hovering over you. They are asking a lot of questions. They want to know your blood type. You aren't able to respond. For one thing, you are in shock. For another, they aren't watching your facial gestures and you have no other way of communicating.

They are now explaining what needs to happen to you. No one seems to notice the fear in your eyes. You hear medical terms you don't understand. You're scared and all alone. Where is your wife? Have they tried to reach her?

Suddenly you are placed on a stretcher and rushed down the hallway into an elevator, then down another hallway and into an operating room. Your last thoughts before the anesthetic takes hold are of…

Who would you think of? Your spouse, your children, your parents, your brothers and sisters, your friends? Or your lawyer, your mechanic, your dentist?

You do survive. The hospital is crowded but they manage to find a semi-private room for you. And they locate your spouse. She comes in several hours after you return from surgery. She immediately understands your terror. You are covered with blood. The needle from the IV tube is already causing noticeable swelling and bruising. Your wife calls a nurse. They respond immediately. They are cooperative and friendly. They didn't expect you to wake up so soon. They were busy elsewhere. The IV tube is adjusted and they give you a warm sponge bath. Eventually you drift off to sleep, comforted by the presence of your wife. At least you are not alone.

When your wife and friends are around, you feel safer and your needs are met. They notice when you are uncomfortable. They do all the little things that make your stay tolerable.

On one occasion you had to contend with an inexperienced intern who insisted on giving you a needle in your arm even though he couldn't find a sizable vein. You were helpless to protest. Your arm became a personal challenge to him. When a colleague from work arrived, it was bruised and bloodied. Within minutes he had your wife on the phone. She spoke to the charge nurse and a notation was made on your chart. It won't happen again, they promised. It doesn't.

What keeps you safe during your hospital stay? Is it hospital rules and regulations? Is it the professional training of medical staff? Is it the nurses and doctors? Or is it friends and family?

Friends and family remove the cloak of anonymity. With them you become a person again. It's not that professional paid care isn't important; it's just that you are more than the sum of your health needs. Make no mistake about it, this move from being an object of service to a real person depends on your relationships.

Why would it be any different for people with disabilities?

It isn't. However, we often make the error of assuming professional paid care is all that is necessary to keep people with disabilities safe and guarantee choice. Programs, professional supports, rules, and regulations have their limitations. Paid service should supplement—not supplant—good, old-fashioned human contact, warmth, and love. ■

Al Etmanski

Choosing a guardian for children under the age of 18

It is difficult to discuss who should take care of our children under the age of 18 should we die unexpectedly.

Unfortunately it does happen, leaving the surviving children, remaining relatives, and friends in legal limbo. The Courts become involved and a judge makes a Custody Order. You cannot assume grandparents, godparents or other choices you think are obvious will automatically be given responsibility. More than 40 per cent of Canadian parents have not legally appointed a guardian for their children.

NOTE Contrary to popular belief, you cannot appoint a guardian for your adult children in your Will. See Step 5 for more details.

You must add a guardianship clause to your Will. One of the toughest decisions faced by parents is determining who to appoint as legal guardian of their minor children. To ease this emotionally difficult process and to prevent further upset, here are some suggestions to assist you in choosing a guardian:

- list your parental values, your aspirations for your children, as well as any religious, financial, or cultural concerns;

- choose the person who comes closest to your parenting style and who would guide your children the way you intend to guide them. A child's aunt or uncle is a common trusted choice, followed by close family friends. Trust in that person's judgment is paramount;

- try to select someone close to your age rather than someone of your parent's generation. Your parents may be excellent grandparents but they may not be able to manage another set of children, especially through the teenage years;

- becoming a guardian adds additional financial as well as emotional responsibilities. In recognition of this, some parents take out a life insurance policy naming the guardian as beneficiary;

- parents of other children with disabilities are a good source of advice. Because of their common bond, parents often choose each other as guardians.

Starlight over the new forest

Starlight over the new forest

in a time without end

the trees are turning to stars

and the stars are turning to trees

the time that went is no longer now

the time to come is no longer still

the time I had is a time of sorrow

the time I stayed to the time I left

the time I took was the thing I lost

the thing I took was the time it cost

I no longer know what the time is

when the time itself is the thing I lost

the thing I took was the time it cost

and now I know what to take from loss.

KIRSTEEN MAIN

Worksheet 9
Supported decision-making

Use this worksheet to organize key decision-making information, issues, and resources that affect the choices and safety of your relative.

A. Checklist
MEDICAL DECISION-MAKING

Who is my relative's doctor? _____

What assistance would they need to make medical decisions? _____

_____

Who would my relative accept to assist with medical decision-making?_____

_____

What aspect of their medical care do I think my relative might understand?_____

_____

What formal arrangements do I need to make to ensure medical care is easily available to my relative? _____

The independent agency that monitors services is:_____

_____

My relative's advocate is: _____

Who would be willing to assist my relative in making lifestyle and personal care decisions?

YES	NO	I have discussed issues of medical consent with my relative's doctor.
YES	NO	The doctor accepts consent from my relative for medical treatment.
YES	NO	The doctor accepts my consent for medical care on my relative's behalf.
YES	NO	My family member has an advocate(s).
YES	NO	The services my relative receives are monitored by a separate and independent agency.
YES	NO	Housing supports are kept separate from other services.
YES	NO	Staff understand and support the importance of family involvement.
YES	NO	Staff understand and welcome the involvement of spouses, friends, and members of the Personal Network.
YES	NO	Service and program staff recognize the importance of offering and respecting my family member's choices.
YES	NO	Family and friends provide support by reviewing services and programs on a regular basis. **NOTE** This is different from the service plans developed by service providers.
YES	NO	Members of the Personal Network are familiar with the personal care issues.

FINANCIAL DECISION-MAKING

YES   NO   My relative has an informal trustee arrangement in place.

YES   NO   My relative has an Enduring Power of Attorney place.

YES   NO   I have set up an income trust.

YES   NO   I have set up a trust (discretionary or non-discretionary).

YES   NO   My relative has an RDSP.

YES   NO   My relative has a bank account.

YES   NO   Withdrawals from that bank account are protected by:

☐ joint signature for withdrawals

☐ my family member is well-known to bank employees

☐ funds in the account are kept to a minimum

☐ don't need to be protected.

B. Information

GENERAL

Who does my relative trust? _____

Who would I trust to assist my relative with decision-making?_____

Who understands my relative's communication style? _____

FINANCIAL DECISIONS

My relative's trustees are:_____

_____

My financial advisors are:_____

_____

My relative has the following bank accounts: _____

_____

Signing authority includes: _____

Who would be willing to assist my relative in making financial decisions?_____

_____

I have asked the following individual to monitor the trust I have set up for my relative: _____

_____

achieving
financial security

wills, trusts,
and the RDSP

Then, when he had flown a while longer,
something brightened toward the north.
It caught his eye, they say.
And then he flew right up against it.

He pushed his mind through
and pulled his body after.

SKAAY, HAIDA POET AND STORYTELLER

Maggie the teacher

The lesson of planning ahead

EARLIER THIS YEAR I developed a heart problem. At the time I thought I was just feeling the effects of middle age (I was 55) and being out of shape. I found myself out of breath after climbing a single flight of steps. My condition worsened to the point that I was waking up in the night gasping for air as if I'd just run a marathon. Cardiac specialists confirmed that, although my heart was quite young, I had developed a seriously leaking mitral valve.

Late that summer, Flora and I travelled to Calgary where I underwent open heart surgery to repair the leaking valve.

It was quite a scare. Although we felt confident that I was in good hands and the surgery would go well, Flora and I reviewed our Wills and talked about our plans. Thankfully, those plans weren't needed and I recovered. The fix was successful and, although I will never be entirely as good as new, my heart is now performing as it should and blood is flowing properly.

The experience has given us some new and direct knowledge of the importance of future planning.

Without Maggie, we would probably be more willing to leave planning until it was almost too late and to trust that our family would adapt to whatever happened as families always do. But Maggie has asked us, through the gift of her being, to be more thoughtful and to be prepared for the time when we will no longer be around. ∎

Achieving financial security: wills, trusts, and the RDSP

This step will provide you with an overview of how to plan for and protect the financial well-being of your family member with a disability both now and in the future. While we are still able, we can help them out in many ways, keeping in mind the rules and other policies imposed by the Assured Income for the Severely Handicapped Program (AISH).

NOTE AISH is the financial assistance that our relatives receive from the provincial government. AISH also provides supplementary benefits such as medical, dental, and special diet allowances. See Resources, page 208 for contact information.

We worry most about what the future will hold. We want to put enough money aside to handle emergencies and unforeseen circumstances. Many people with disabilities live at or below the poverty line. We don't want our relatives to just get by. Simply existing is not enough; we also want our family members to have a good life.

Most of us are not sufficiently wealthy to leave enough money in our estate to cover the costs of everything that our family members might possibly need. Until recently, there were limited options or tools we could use to deal with this challenge. If our family members relied on government benefits, there was little we could do to supplement their income without it being clawed back by the provincial government.

Step five highlights

This chapter highlights the key tools at your disposal to plan for the financial security of your relative. These include:

- Will and estate planning
- discretionary trusts (also referred to as Henson Trusts)
- the RDSP.

This information will help with your preparation but is no substitute for legal advice.

Fortunately this is starting to change in Alberta, where the government has recently committed to assisting individuals build up savings. Some penalties and disincentives are being eliminated. For example, the money received from the RDSP will NOT be clawed back (see detailed discussion on the RDSP in Section Two below, and for ongoing updates, please visit www.rdsp.com or www.rdspresource.ca).

These changes signify that we are approaching a new partnership between families and government, a partnership based on shared responsibility which acknowledges the commitment that families have always made to the safety and well-being of their relatives with disabilities.

This chapter is divided into two main sections:

SECTION ONE: Wills, Trusts, and Estate Planning

SECTION TWO: The Registered Disability Savings Plan (RDSP).

The information contained in these two sections will:

- provide you with general information on drafting a Will and planning your estate
- highlight the importance of trusts, particularly discretionary trusts
- introduce you to the Registered Disability Savings Plan (RDSP)
- discuss the relationship among government benefits, the RDSP, and discretionary trusts
- overall, help you plan for the financial security of your relative.

Assuming financial security for your relative need not be complicated, particularly if you have thought through the issues raised in the preceding steps. Yes, it's technical but Worksheet 10 on page 168 will help. Once you have completed it, there are plenty of good lawyers, accountants, financial and estate planners, and wealth management specialists to help you finalize your plans.

This chapter won't replace the need to make some tough choices. The professionals you will choose are highly skilled but they rely on the clarity of your vision, your plans, and your details in order to make the right plan for your family.

Fortunately you are not alone. You can use PLAN as a back-up resource. Our advice has been sifted through the experiences of thousands of individuals and families we have supported over more than 20 years. We've learned from them all. Even those of us with little disposable income or limited assets can still leave something to help our relatives.

We pass on this accumulated wisdom knowing that being better prepared will:

- save you time and money

- assist you in selecting the right course for your relative

- make it easier to complete your Will

- leave you with peace of mind.

You'll feel a great sense of accomplishment and relief when you've finally done it!

Wills, trusts, and estate planning

Do not be intimidated by legal language. All professions have their jargon. Some of the key words and phrases you'll encounter in this section are summarized in Demystifying Definitions on page 166.

In praise of the imperfect Will

You've heard the facts before. Too many Canadians die without a Will. Many others die with a Will that's out-of-date. In a recent Environics survey of 1,000 adults, 31 per cent of respondents said they have never broached the subject of life insurance with their partners; 59 per cent said they had never even thought about it. You want to avoid joining their ranks. But you don't have all the answers. You still need to work out a few more details. You're just about there... maybe after reading this chapter.

Well, we're sorry to disappoint you. This chapter will not help you create the perfect Will. Neither will any other book, or person for that matter. So don't make the same mistake too many others have made. Don't wait for something that will never happen.

Now is the time to develop and execute the "imperfect" Will. It is one of the biggest gifts you can give to your family and to yourself. We feel so strongly about this we might call our next book, "In Praise of Imperfection."

What's so great about perfection anyway? Where did we get the grandiose illusion that we humans can either be perfect or get things perfect? The perfect meal or the perfect day? Maybe. But the perfect body, perfect looks, and the perfect job while living in the perfect house? Not likely. Perfection is an illusion which adds unnecessary pressure and can make us feel guilty for never measuring up. Surely, absolute perfection is the job of divine personalities, beyond the scope of mere mortals. Few, if any of us, ever attain these standards. Yet we still manage to get on with our lives.

And that's precisely what we want you to do with your Will. Get on with it! Preparing and completing the imperfect Will is not the least you can do, it's the best you can do.

Beginning to create your Will and estate plan

Before you create your Will, you must be clear about the details. Every family situation is unique. You are going to rely on your family after you are gone, so it's a good idea to discuss things with them now. If the person you want to be your executor is intimidated by lawyers or has never invested money, now is the time to find out.

There are other valuable resource people you might consider talking to: extended family, friends, members of your relative's Personal Network, other families in similar circumstances, and so on.

In our experience, it helps families clarify their objectives by talking to others in similar circumstances. The more open and forthright your discussions are, the clearer your objectives will be. This will make for a more meaningful and more efficient relationship with your lawyer, accountant, and estate planning specialist. When seeking advice on estate planning, tax planning, or wealth management strategies, see Questions to ask an Advisor on page 139.

Nine key objectives

Most people want their Will and estate plan to:

1. pay their debts, taxes, and other liabilities

2. provide a separate independent income for their spouse

3. distribute their assets according to their wishes

4. maximize the size of their estate for their children

5. protect the financial security of their relative with a disability
   NOTE The RDSP and discretionary trusts are your basic tools for this.

6. ensure that the appropriate estate and disability trustees are in place

7. ensure that there is a guardian for their children under the age of 18.

> Surely the true definition of courage is to do the thing you are afraid to do.
>
> GEORGIA BINNIE CLARK

Tips from Jack Collins for securing the future

Jack Collins—one of PLAN's co-founders and a co-author of this book—knows much about the legal and financial elements of securing the future. After he retired, he dedicated his time to learning everything possible about the technical aspects of will and estate planning and how they can be coordinated with government benefits. Although he is a lay person, many lawyers, financial and estate planners rely on his insights and advice.

His credibility among families is legendary. They like his plain speaking, no nonsense style. They trust him because he is one of them. Culled from his vault of expertise and its application to thousands of families, here are tips from the master!

- Get a basic Will as quickly as possible. I have seen what happens when a parent dies without a Will.

- Review your Will every two years and update it when something in your life changes. Additions and amendments (called codicils) are not costly.

- Life insurance is a good way to finance a discretionary trust. For a small monthly premium you can finance a policy. After you die the proceeds can be placed tax free—and without probate costs—into your family member's discretionary trust.

- Appoint executors and trustees who will outlive you—in other words, appoint someone younger than you—and appoint alternates just in case.

- The year of your death will likely be your highest income year because most investments are deemed sold on the day of your death and any remaining RRSPs or RRIFs get added to your income. Tax and estate planning—including donations to charity—will reduce the tax bite.

- Most of us want the trust capital as well as income to go entirely to our relative. To do so, your trust document must specifically exclude the "even handed rule" so the trustee(s) do not have to consider the rights of residual beneficiaries. If such permission is granted within the trust document, then the trustees will be encouraged to spend down the capital as well as income. Please consult your lawyer on this technical point.

- Grandparents often look for ways to help secure the future of their grandchildren. Suggest they create a discretionary trust—or contribute to an RDSP—for their grandchild with a disability.

  NOTE the generosity of a grandparent in setting up a trust (either discretionary or non-discretionary) for a grandchild may result in that grandchild's AISH benefits being eliminated. Grandparents are cautioned to thoroughly discuss this eventuality with both their lawyer and the parents of the grandchild that they are intending to "benefit" before creating any trust.

8. avoid delays, family strife, needless taxation, costly legal challenges, probate fees, and government involvement

9. allocate a portion of their estate to the charities and causes they are passionate about.

Basic questions about Wills, trusts, estates, and the RDSP

Once you've added your own personalized objectives to the nine general objectives described above and you are comfortable, well, reasonably comfortable, with your answers, you are ready for the technical solutions. Here are some questions and answers to start you on your way.

NOTE For a complete list of legal terms, see "Demystifying definitions that could definitely derail you" on page 166.

WHAT IS A WILL? A Will is the legal document that tells people what to do with your estate. It helps makes life easier for those left behind by providing a plan for them to follow and by naming who is in charge.

WHAT IS ESTATE PLANNING? Estate planning is quite a broad term. It includes such things as:

- preparing your Will

- preparing Powers of Attorney and Personal Directives or personal declarations about end of life decisions

- deciding upon issues such as executor and trustee appointment, and finding ways to minimize probate fees

- calculating your estate needs and determining the amount of life insurance needed to meet those needs

- looking at strategies to reduce income taxes at death

- advising about a trust for you or a trust for your relative with a disability.

WHAT ARE THE BASIC THINGS I NEED TO THINK ABOUT? During the course of designing your Will and planning your estate you will need to:

> Family is not an important thing, it's everything.
>
> MICHAEL J. FOX

- appoint one or more personal representatives (or "executors") to ensure that the instructions in your Will are carried out

- divide your estate among family (spouse and children), charities, and others

- create a trust, usually a discretionary trust, for your relative with a disability and identify a trustee and perhaps co-trustee(s) to manage the trust

- appoint a guardian for your children who are under the age of 18 years.

WHAT HAPPENS IF I DIE WITHOUT A WILL? If you die without a Will, provincial laws set out how your estate will be distributed. Under the *Intestate Succession Act* (Alberta), the Court will appoint an administrator who will divide your estate. This means you will have no control over how your estate is divided. You will not be able to protect the inheritance you want to leave to your relative with a disability.

The funds for your relative may be held in trust by the Public Trustee for Alberta until they turn 18 years, at which time they will receive their total inheritance outright.

NOTE This situation may disqualify the beneficiary from receiving AISH assistance.

If you die without a Will and you have children who are under the age of 18, and there is no surviving parent who is the legal guardian, then the Public Guardian for Alberta may become guardian of those children (see Is your child under the age of 18? on page 165).

HOW MUCH WILL MY CHILDREN GET IF I DIE WITHOUT A WILL? If you die without a Will, the *Intestate Succession Act* (Alberta) and the *Dependants Relief Act* (Alberta) impact the distribution of your estate. The *Intestate Succession Act* directs that:

- the first $40,000 of your property goes to your spouse

- if you die leaving one child, one-half of the remainder of your estate goes to your spouse and one-half goes to your child

> If you die without a Will, you have no control over how your estate is divided.

- if you die leaving more than one child, one-third of the remainder of your estate goes to your spouse and the remaining two-thirds is divided equally among your children

- your next-of-kin will have to go to Court to be allowed to deal with your estate.

NOTE The *Dependants Relief Act* requires that your Will provide adequately for your dependents, which could include not only your spouse but also your adult dependent children as well.

The definition of "child" in the *Dependants Relief Act* includes your children who are under 18 years of age and those children who are over 18 years of age and unable by reason of mental or physical disability to earn a livelihood. This means that the law requires you to "adequately provide" for your adult dependent children through your Will.

If a spouse or child feels you have not provided adequately for them in your Will, then they can ask the Court to change your Will to get a larger share of the estate. This must be done within six months of probate. There is no set formula which is used to determine what would constitutes "proper share" for the maintenance and support of a dependant; the Court is entitled to take into account all matters that should be "fairly taken into account."

The funds for your minor children may be held in trust by the Public Trustee for Alberta until your children reach the age of majority unless a trusteeship application is made by the surviving spouse to manage the child's property.

WHO IS THE PUBLIC TRUSTEE? The Public Trustee is responsible for protecting the interests of children who are under the age of 18 years. Your executor is required to provide estate and trust accounts that are presented for Court approval to the Public Trustee whenever a minor or unborn person has a vested or future interest in an estate.

AISH ASSISTANCE: AISH is a provincial government program that provides financial assistance as well as supplements such as medical, dental, optical, pharmaceutical and special diet benefits to people with

> The mind is
> not a vessel
> to be filled,
> but a hearth
> to be lighted.
>
> IRENE PARLBY

disabilities. To be eligible, a person must meet the required definition of disability and financial criteria. For contact information, see Resources on page 208.

At the time of writing, a single person on AISH may receive a monthly living allowance up to $1,188, together with health benefits (prescription drugs, optical and dental services) and other discretionary personal benefits.

Once people are 18 years of age, they are entitled to AISH if:

- they are Canadian citizens or permanent residents who are ordinarily resident in Alberta

- they have a (prolonged) severe handicap (as defined by the AISH Act)

- they have less than $100,000 in non-exempt assets; that is, things a person owns including money, property, and investments **NOTE** The $100,000 asset limit does not include the value of exempt assets such as their primary residence

- they earn income which below the guidelines established by the regulations to the AISH Act.

If an individual on AISH has assets of more than $100,000 in non-exempt assets, then they may be cut off until those assets are worth less than $100,000. There are, however, a number of exempt assets including a:

- principal residence (and reasonable household items)

- vehicle (and a second vehicle, if adapted to accommodate the individual's handicap)

- Registered Disability Savings Plan

- locked-in retirement account.

We don't have to choose; we have to talk to each other about what concerns us deeply.

HAROLD RHENISCH

HOW AISH IS AFFECTED BY INCOME

EARNED INCOME

Persons on AISH are able to work and earn income. The AISH Regulations contain a detailed listing of income exemption calculations for individuals, their spouses, and dependent children. AISH benefits are clawed back, or reduced, based on the amount of non-exempt income earned by an individual and their family unit per month. The AISH Regulations should be carefully reviewed to determine your relative's own income exemption entitlements.

OTHER INCOME

Other sources of income are also taken in account when determining both eligibility and the amount of income support to be provided to the individual. Examples of such income include:

- tax-exempt employment, self-employment, or pension income of a treaty Indian

- trust income, as deemed by the Director appointed under the AISH Act, payable to a beneficiary under a trust.

There are several income exemptions, most notably: benefits received under the AISH Act; income for the benefit of a dependent child; RRSP withdrawals; and payments under an RDSP.

HOW AISH IS AFFECTED BY INCOME SUCH AS AN INHERITANCE
If people on AISH receive income from an inheritance, a life insurance payout, or other financial windfall, then their amount of assistance may be reduced or suspended until they have only $100,000 left. If the person on AISH has the capacity to enter into a contract, then they can place up to $100,000 in a trust and up to $200,000 in an RDSP without affecting their AISH eligibility.

WHAT BENEFITS DO MY RELATIVES QUALIFY FOR ONCE THEY
TURN 65? When your relative reaches the age of 65, they will move from provincial income assistance to federal seniors benefits: Old Age Security (OAS) and Guaranteed Income Supplement (GIS). Together, these two benefits provide approximately the same amount as AISH income.

I wear my shadows where they are harder to see, but they follow me everywhere. I guess that should tell me I'm traveling toward light.

BRUCE COCKBURN

Old Age Security is not asset or income tested. This means that all senior Canadians receive a monthly amount whether or not they have assets or income.

The Guaranteed Income Supplement is the federal government program that helps low-income seniors. It is not asset-tested; it is, however, income-tested. Any income that seniors receive is clawed back at 50 per cent including income from a trust.

The good news for holders of RDSPs is that the Guaranteed Income Supplement will not be affected by income received from an RDSP. In other words, RDSP income is exempt.

CAN I SET UP AN RDSP AND A TRUST? Yes you can. There are benefits to each and you may want to do both. See page 159 for a comparison. In general, the RDSP is designed to build savings and can be used while parents are still alive. Trusts are typically designed to manage the inheritance you leave for your relative. A trust in your Will becomes operational only after you die. Trusts can also be created as inter-vivos trusts that take effect while you are still alive.
NOTE If a grandparent sets up a trust, then the money may become available before the parent dies.

WHY SHOULD I SET UP A TRUST? A trust (preferably a discretionary trust) may be advisable for many reasons:

- to help your relative with a disability during their lifetime and then to pass on funds that remain to another generation or a chosen charity
- to protect a vulnerable relative from being taken advantage of by those with bad motives and also those with good intentions but limited skills or judgment
- to provide ongoing financial management of assets
- to take advantage of special tax treatment
- to give some protection of assets if a relative goes through a marriage breakdown or has creditors.

WHAT PROVISIONS SHOULD I ADD TO MY WILL TO BENEFIT MY RELATIVE WITH A DISABILITY?

You can set up a trust in your Will for the person with a disability. The best course of action is to talk to a lawyer who has expertise in providing Wills and estate advice to families of people with disabilities.

There are two common trusts used by families of people with disabilities: non-discretionary trusts (also called government regulated trusts, inheritance trusts, or shelter trusts) and discretionary trusts (also called Henson Trusts).

NON-DISCRETIONARY TRUSTS

A non-discretionary trust means that the beneficiary of the trust can request payment of funds out of the trust and the trustee has no discretion. The trustee must pay out the requested fund.

A non-discretionary trust can be set up in two ways. One way is by a friend or relative of the individual with a disability. The other way is by the individual with a disability, as long as the person has the capacity to manage property.

Regardless of who sets up the trust, as long as the amount of money in the non-discretionary trust is under $100,000 it will not be treated as an asset for individuals on AISH. It is important to note that these trusts are reviewed by the provincial government and need to be designed properly in order to be approved. For example, there must be at least one trustee in addition to the beneficiary.

If the total of the capital contribution and income generated by the non-discretionary trust exceeds $100,000, then the individual may no longer be eligible for AISH. Funds from the trust can be spent on disability-related costs without affecting the individual's entitlement to AISH.

DISCRETIONARY TRUSTS

Most families of people with disabilities choose to set up a discretionary trust in their Will. To do this, you appoint a trustee—and possibly co-trustee(s)—as the person(s) who will be in charge of the trust. You give the trustee(s) the discretion—or power—to decide when and how much of the trust fund will be used from time to time for the

---

Lost and Found

Man finds gold.
Man loses gold.
Man finds time.
Man loses hair.
Man finds dream.
Man loses dream.
Man finds laughter.
Man loses time.
Man finds
meaning to life.
Man loses life.

TOM KONYVES

beneficiary, in this case your relative with a disability. Your trustee(s) can then gauge your relative's changing needs over time and adjust disbursements accordingly.

HOW DOES A DISCRETIONARY TRUST AFFECT MY RELATIVE? In many provinces and territories throughout Canada, there is no ceiling on the amount that can be placed in a discretionary trust (also called a "Henson Trust") without adversely affecting AISH-equivalent benefits. This is because funds held in a discretionary trust are not considered to be either owned or controlled by your relative (those funds are actually owned by the trust and controlled by the trustee(s)) and are therefore not included in calculating your relative's personal net worth for the purpose of determining your relative's entitlement to AISH-equivalent benefits. This, however, is not the case in Alberta.

A WORD OF CAUTION ABOUT DISCRETIONARY TRUSTS AND AISH BENEFITS

Under Alberta's AISH legislation, the Director appointed under the AISH Act (the Director) has the ability to deem that all funds which are held in a discretionary trust belong to your relative. Accordingly, if there are funds (or non-exempt assets) which are held in a discretionary trust for the benefit of your relative which are valued at more than $100,000, the Director could exercise its discretion to deem that your relative is entitled to receive all of those funds/assets, thereby disentitling your relative from receiving AISH benefits until such time as those funds/assets are worth less than $100,000.

It remains to be seen, however, whether the Director will use its power in this way and, if so, how effective it would be if a family were to challenge such decision. Given the fact that the Alberta government has recently approved RDSPs as an exempt asset and therefore appears to be not only acknowledging, but actually encouraging families to provide for and secure their relative's financial future, it would seem counter-intuitive and therefore unlikely, that the Director would actually exercise its discretion to, in effect, actively discourage families from doing so.

While we remain hopeful that the Alberta government will recognize this problem and revisit this legislative anomaly in the near future, it is recommended that, for the time being, parents and their advisors develop their estate plans with the expectation that the use of a discretionary trust may not save the assets in the trust from the application of the AISH claw back rules.

This does not, however, mean that a discretionary trust has no place as a planning tool; a discretionary trust can and still provides one of the most flexible estate planning tools available to families who wish to provide a financial safety net for their relatives. The discretionary trust still has a valuable place in implementing your estate planning objectives in Alberta, but it must be carefully implemented in order to avoid (or, at least, reduce) the possibility of the elimination of AISH benefits. In preparing your estate plan, you should seek advice from a knowledgeable lawyer who is familiar with this area of estate planning; they may be able to suggest alternative strategies and variations on discretionary trusts as a possible means of structuring your discretionary trust without adversely affecting your relative's AISH benefits.

The AISH Act and Regulations change from time to time. Check the Resources section on page 208 for contact information.

WHAT HAPPENS TO THE MONEY LEFT IN THE TRUST WHEN THE BENEFICIARY DIES? When you set up a trust, you must also identify who will get what is left in the trust when the beneficiary dies. This could be the beneficiary's spouse, children, siblings, other family members, charities, or anyone else.

You should be careful to avoid a potential conflict of interest when you choose the trustees of the trust you establish for your family member.

Who inherits the remainder of the trust? If the person inheriting the residual amount of the trust (the residual beneficiary) is the only person responsible for making spending decisions when the primary beneficiary dies, then there is a potential conflict of interest. One solution is to appoint co-trustees. We suggest you discuss this matter with your lawyer to avoid the Office of the Public Trustee trying to vary the Will.

WHAT DOES A TRUSTEE DO? The trustee:

- manages or looks after the trust assets
- makes sure your relative receives trust benefits according to your wishes.

If you decide to set up a trust for your relative, you will need to name the trustee in your Will. Choosing a trustee is one of the most crucial decisions you will make about future planning. The person you choose may have responsibilities as a trustee for 40 years or more.

It is a good idea to have more than one trustee. For example, you may want to have two trustees and two alternates in case the original trustees cannot act or cannot agree. It's also a good idea to choose a trustee who is much younger than you in age. You want them to live as long as your relative does!

WHO SHOULD BE A TRUSTEE? You may want to have one trustee with financial skills and a co-trustee who has a personal relationship with your relative. Their skill sets may be different and may complement each other. One trustee might make investment decisions, keep accounts, manage tax returns, and so on. The other trustee, a sibling or friend, would be in a better position to advise on how to spend trust funds.

> Choosing a trustee is one of the most crucial decisions you will make about future planning.

You may consider using a respected trust company as one of the trustees. Some families use a trust company as one trustee and a relative or family friend as the other trustee. The trust company can make sure there is experienced financial help to invest and manage the trust assets. The relative, friend, or Personal Network member makes sure the funds are spent in the best interests of your relative.

If you name a person as a trustee, then you should also name a successor in case the first person dies, moves, or is otherwise not willing or able to continue. It is best if the trustees are people your relative knows and likes. The trustees and your relative will likely be involved with one another for a long time. A good relationship between them will benefit everyone.

At least one of the trustees should live close to your relative. If a trustee has close contact with your relative, they will understand the needs of your relative better.

WHAT ARE THE DUTIES OF A TRUSTEE? The duties of a trustee include:

- deciding how and when to spend funds
- making payments to or for the beneficiary
- managing investments and safekeeping assets
- coordinating any maintenance/repairs of real estate
- preparing trust tax returns
- maintaining records of the trust
- reporting to the beneficiary about the trust.

NOTE you can direct your trustees to consider certain expenditures, for example, to purchase a home for your relative.

IN ALBERTA, DO EXECUTORS AND TRUSTEES GET PAID? You can state in your Will or in a contract (that is incorporated by reference in your Will) how much your executor is to be compensated. If you don't say how much they should be paid, then Court recognized guidelines may be applied. The fees that trustees charge are influenced by the magnitude of the estate and the amount of time, effort, and skill that has been required of them while acting as your trustee.

NOTE If your executor is also administering a trust, then they may be entitled to additional compensation.

Where there's a Will, there's a way.

WHAT INVESTMENT POWERS SHOULD I GIVE MY TRUSTEE? Trustees are limited by law to investments that a prudent person would make. You may give them greater investment powers but you must specify it in your Will. Be sure to discuss this with your lawyer.

CAN I APPOINT A GUARDIAN FOR MY CHILD IN MY WILL? If you have children under the age of 18, you should appoint a guardian for them in your Will. You should also appoint alternates in case the first is not able to accept.

You cannot appoint a guardian for an adult child even if they have a severe disability; however, you can express a wish in your Will that supports an individual to be a guardian of your adult child should this become necessary.

WHO SHOULD BE THE EXECUTOR OF MY WILL? The executor is the person who makes sure that the instructions in your Will are carried out after you die. Often people appoint their spouse as their executor, but you may need to appoint someone else or someone jointly with your spouse. You should also appoint alternates in the event the original executor is unable to fulfill the responsibilities of executor. It is recommended that you discuss the proposed appointments with each of the executors you choose before you name them in your Will.

If you have set up a trust in your Will, usually the executor and alternate executor will be the same as your trustees and alternate trustees. However, in some cases, for example where there is a business to be managed, you may wish to have different executors and trustees. Talk to your lawyer about this.

WHICH OF MY ASSETS DO NOT FORM PART OF MY ESTATE AND PASS OUTSIDE THE WILL? Any assets held in joint tenancy with another person pass directly to that person on your death and are not governed by your Will. For example, a home and bank accounts held in joint tenancy with your spouse go directly to your spouse on your death.

Life insurance policies with a designated adult beneficiary pass outside the Will directly to that beneficiary.

RRSPs and RRIFs with a designated adult beneficiary pass directly to that beneficiary.

Quite often when a spouse dies, most of the family assets are held in one of these ways and pass directly to the surviving spouse. Assets which pass outside your Will save probate fees.

Assets held in trusts that have been established prior to your death are also not part of your estate.

Be sure to consult your lawyer about putting assets in joint tenancy with your children or anyone else as there are dangers as well as benefits in so doing.

SHOULD I MAKE A GIFT TO A CHARITY THROUGH MY WILL?

Estates often have a lot of taxes to pay. This is because any funds in RRSPs and RRIFs are considered income in the year of a person's death. Other assets are deemed to be sold in the year of the death. Tax is payable by the estate on this income and any earned capital gains.

When you make a gift to a registered charity through your Will, your estate receives a charitable tax receipt which can be used to reduce the income tax that has to be paid.

If you have supported charities while you are alive, you may wish to consider supporting charities through your Will. You should discuss these wishes with your estate planning professionals. Most charities have planned giving programs set up to be able to respond to inquiries about leaving a charity a gift through your Will. You are also able to leave charities gifts of life insurance, property, RRSPs or RRIFs, as well as through many other innovative vehicles. When you have decided on your charity or charities of choice, you should consider contacting them to discuss the gift.

CAN I MAKE A GIFT TO PLAN IN MY WILL? Many families appreciate the work that PLAN does and support its continued financial independence by making a charitable gift or by leaving a bequest through their Will.

The professionals you choose will be highly skilled but they still need the clarity of your vision to make the right plan for your family.

Please see Resources for contact information for LACL, PLAN Calgary, and PLAN Edmonton to discuss specific programs that you would like to support through your estate. Any request for anonymity will, of course, be respected.

CAN I LEAVE MY RRSP AND RRIFS TO A RELATIVE WITH A DISABILITY? If you have a lot of assets in RRSPs or RRIFs, you may want to consider leaving them specifically for a son or daughter or grandchild with a disability when you die. If you do leave these assets to a child or grandchild with a disability, then the federal government provides a tax deduction equal to the total amount of the RRSP or RRIF going to that beneficiary. This means your estate wouldn't have to pay any taxes on these assets.

This can, however, create two problems. First, your relative may be vulnerable and, therefore, not able to manage that asset. Secondly, depending upon the amount involved, the asset may adversely affect your relative's AISH eligibility and benefits. However, if the amount is less than $300,000, they may be able to put the funds into a trust ($100,000) and RDSP ($200,000) and not lose their AISH eligibility and benefits.

The federal government has indicated that they plan to permit funds from the RRSP or RIFF to be passed on to a trust but the legislation is not yet in force. However, RRSPs and RIFs can now be "rolled over" to an RDSP (see page 150).

We recommend you discuss this option with your lawyer or check with PLAN for the most current information.

WHAT IS PROBATE? Probate is the name of the legal process that confirms your last Will. Normally it is the job of your executor to file your Will for probate with the Surrogate Court of Alberta and pay the applicable probate fees. This process usually takes anywhere from a few weeks to a few months. Until your executor receives the grant of probate, assets of your estate cannot be released.

Probate fees in Alberta are based on the net value of the estate property located in Alberta and are currently as follows:

When seeking advice on estate planning, tax planning, or wealth management strategies ask:

1. What is your experience, knowledge, and training?
2. How long have you been doing this?
3. How are you compensated for your advice?
4. Have you worked with other families who have a child with a disability?

$10,000	or	under	$25
$10,000	to	$25,000	$100
$25,000	to	$125,000	$200
$125,000	to	$250,000	$300
Over		$250,000	$400

UNDER WHAT CIRCUMSTANCES SHOULD A PERSON WITH A DISABILITY SET UP A TRUST OR MAKE A WILL? Many individuals with disabilities do establish trusts and make Wills. This will become even more important for people with RDSPs. The law has legal tests which all individuals, with or without a disability, must meet in order to place their assets in a trust or execute a Will. For example, in order to create a Will, an individual must know what a Will is and know and understand what their assets and liabilities are and their value. If an individual cannot meet the legal tests required, then they would not be able to settle a trust or make a Will at that time.

An individual's capacity, however, is not a static thing. An individual without the legal capacity to execute a Will may, six months later, have the requisite capacity. Furthermore, lawyers vary in their understanding and appreciation of capacity of people with disabilities. You may find it useful to consult with legal professionals who have familiarity and experience working with individuals with disabilities. Your local PLAN office, or a trusted community organization, will have a list of experienced legal professionals.

Seeking advice from professionals

There are a variety of experienced professionals in the future planning business. There is no substitute for good professional help. There are lawyers, financial planners, accountants, and trust companies that have special expertise in helping plan for the needs of children and relatives with disabilities. They can help you maximize the size of your estate, save you money, and ensure that your instructions are written in proper legal language. They are guided by principles of confidentiality, prudent administration, and sound judgment.

As with all professional services, be a cautious consumer. Always ask the professional their estimated fee before hiring them. You can also ask other parents or check with your local PLAN affiliate.

Life changes

No matter how exhaustive your preparation and thorough your study, your Will may never be complete and will never be perfect. While preparing for this chapter, we were consulting with one of the most prestigious estate planners in the country. He interrupted our interview to visit his lawyer. After over 35 years in the business, he is still revising his Will!

Expect to revise your Will as life changes. The act of revision is relatively painless and inexpensive. And the peace of mind is incalculable.

Eight tips in making your Will if you have a relative with a disability

1. Complete the Will Planning Worksheet beginning on page 168. This will give you an idea of your assets and help you make decisions.

2. Decide how you want your estate distributed. For example: all to spouse and when spouse dies, split among children in equal shares.

3. Appoint an executor and alternate executor.

4. Decide if you want to set up a trust for your family member with a disability. Ensure there is no conflict of interest. If you do decide to set up a trust who will be:

- the trustee
- the beneficiary of the trust when your relative dies.

5. Be aware that the following pass outside the Will:

- life insurance with a designated beneficiary
- RRSPs and RRIFs with a designated beneficiary
- assets held in joint tenancy.

6. If you have children under 18 years of age, decide whom you will appoint as their guardian.

7. Take all this information to a lawyer who has experience in Wills and estates for families and individuals with disabilities. Ask the lawyer to explain the tax and legal implications of your decisions.

8. Discuss your draft Will with your trustees.

The registered disability savings plan (RDSP)

Following more than eight years of federal advocacy by PLAN, Canada became the first country in the world to implement an RDSP. As a result, both the Government of Canada and the Government of Alberta have now made it easier for families to secure the financial future of their relatives.

The RDSP is a powerful tool for securing the financial well-being of your relative. Anyone can contribute to an RDSP. And the funds grow on a tax-deferred basis. In most situations, the federal government will assist by generously matching your contributions (see discussion on Grant and Bond below). **The RDSP will NOT affect provincial disability benefits.**

The RDSP is a tax-deferred savings plan. It is estimated that 500,000 Canadians with disabilities are eligible. An RDSP can be purchased at most financial institutions in Canada. Visit www.rdsp.com for a current list of financial institutions offering an RDSP.

Maximum lifetime contributions to an RDSP are $200,000. This does not include the matching Grants and Bonds received from the federal government or any income earned from investments.

Anyone can make a contribution: parents, grandparents, other family members, friends, agencies, foundations, and so on. The contributions are not tax-deductible and once contributed into the RDSP, they become the asset of the beneficiary of the RDSP.

When a contribution is made, the federal government through the Canada Disability Savings Grant will add as much as three times the contribution to your relative's plan. How much, however, depends on

> What a blessing it is that we can so dream into life the things we desire!
>
> LUCY MAUD MONTGOMERY

Income thresholds

The income thresholds of $83,088 for the Disability Savings Grant and $24,183 and $41,544 for the Disability Savings Bond, respectively, are 2011 figures. These numbers are indexed and will change over time. For the most current information, please visit www.hrsdc.gc.ca.

How to maximize your RDSP grants

With the combined benefits of tax-deferred growth and compounded income, the RDSP is a powerful planning tool for parents. For example, a family has a nine year old daughter named Erica, and their annual income is under $83,088. If $1,500 is contributed annually for 20 years ($1,500 x 20 = $30,000), then Erica will have nearly $350,000 in savings by the time she turns 40. At that time, a life annuity could be purchased providing her with an estimated $1,500 per month. For detailed examples of how the RDSP can work for your family, please refer to the scenarios on page 155.

your family income, or the beneficiary's income if they are 19 years or older. If annual income is below $83,088, the matching is better than if annual income is over $83,088. Either way, the Canada Disability Savings Grant allows you to multiply a contribution and it will grow on a tax-deferred basis.

In addition, if annual net income is under $24,183, then the beneficiary is eligible for the full amount of Canada Disability Savings Bond. If income is between $24,183 and $41,544, then a pro-rated portion will be received. The lifetime maximum Bond that can be received is $20,000. When payments are received from the RDSP, the portion of the RDSP that is the Grant or the Bond—plus the accumulated investment income—is taxable in the beneficiary's hands, not in the hands of the contributor.

An RDSP is considered an exempt asset by AISH. In other words, having an RDSP will not affect your relative's AISH benefits. In fact, RDSP funds can be used at any time for any purpose without affecting AISH benefits.

Income from an RDSP is also exempt from claw backs against the Guaranteed Income Supplement. This is important because once your relative turns 65 years of age, they move from AISH to Old Age Security and Guaranteed Income Supplement. Currently, any income— except payments from an RDSP— is clawed back from the Guaranteed Income Supplement at a rate of 50 per cent.

Both levels of government have sent a clear message to families: they trust people with disabilities and their families and there is no need to interfere with how families spend their money and how they live their lives.

Basic Elements of the RDSP

If your relative is a resident of Canada under age 60 and eligible for the Disability Tax Credit, then they are eligible to open an RDSP. Qualification for the Disability Tax Credit requires a "severe and prolonged impairment."

For details, see Income Tax Form T2201 available from the Canada Revenue Agency website or by calling Canada Revenue Agency at 1-800-959-2221. If you would like assistance in applying for the Disability Tax Credit, the RDSP Resource Centre, a PLAN partner, can provide assistance. See the Resource section on page 212 for contact information.

Features of the RDSP

Features of the RDSP include:

- contributions of up to $200,000 can be made to your relative's RDSP

- Grant and Bond entitlements can be carried forward for up to 10 years

- the RDSP grows on a tax-deferred basis

- a beneficiary can have only one RDSP

- contributions can be made by anyone or any organization including, for example, but not limited to: the beneficiary or any family member, friend, a foundation, or a service club

- contributions to an RDSP can be made until the end of the year in which your relative turns 59. Payments from the RDSP must begin once your relative reaches the age of 60, but may begin before at the holder's discretion

When we focus on our standard expectations for behaviour and communication in our fast-paced, super technological world, we may miss opportunities to know and understand people who are likely among the most patient and best listeners on the planet.

MARTHA LEARY

- the portion of the RDSP made up of government contributions (that is, the Grant and Bond) and investment income is taxed in the hands of the your relative when withdrawn; any personal contributions (including those made by friends and family) will not be taxed

- payments from the RDSP can begin at any time. If the plan has received the Grant or the Bond, payments should not begin until 10 years after the last Grant and Bond was received to avoid repayment of the holdback amount (see discussion on the Grant and the Bond below)

- one-time payments of any size are permitted when family contributions exceed government contributions

- an RDSP can be opened at most financial institutions and through many independent financial planners

- an RDSP can be moved from one financial institution to another

- an RDSP can be invested in most financial instruments; for example, T-bills, GICs, bonds, stocks, or mutual funds

- RRSPs can be "rolled over" to the RDSPs of sons, daughters, and grandchildren, resulting in significant tax savings (see page 150).

Having an RDSP will not affect your relative's government benefits.

The Canada Disability Savings Grant

The Canada Disability Savings Grant will provide matching contributions of as much as three times your private contributions to a lifetime maximum of $70,000. The maximum annual Grant is $3,500. Your relative can receive the Grant until December 31 of the year in which they turn 49 years old.

Features of the Canada Disability Savings Grant

Features of the Canada Disability Savings Grant include:

- if annual net income is under $83,088, then the Grant is equal to three times the first $500 of RDSP contribution; for example, a $500 contribution is matched by a $1,500 Grant. The Grant on the next $1,000 of RDSP contribution is two times the contribution; for example, a $1,000 contribution is matched by a $2,000 Grant (see chart on page 148)

- the maximum Grant that can be received in a year is $3,500

- the lifetime maximum Grant is $70,000

- if annual net income is over $83,088, then the first $1,000 is matched one-to-one; for example, a $1,000 contribution is matched by a $1,000 Grant

- the amount of matching Grant or Bond your relative is eligible for depends on your family's annual net income each year until December 31st of the year that your relative turns 18 years old. Starting January 1st of the year that your relative turns 19 years old, their net income is used

- effective 2011, you can claim the Grant for previous years (see New Carry Forward Rules, page 149)

- if payments from an RDSP are made within 10 years of receiving the Canada Disability Savings Grant, then the holdback amount (the total of Grant or Bond received within the preceding 10 years) must be repaid. To avoid repayment of the holdback amount, no payments should be made from the RDSP for 10 years after the last Grant or Bond is received. For example, if you make 20 years of contributions to your relative's RDSP and it receives matching Grants each year, then payments should not begin for 10 more years

- if you set up an RDSP for your relative and choose NOT to receive the Canada Disability Savings Grant and the Canada Disability Savings Bond, then the 10-year rule referred to above does NOT apply.

Canada Disability Savings Bond

The Canada Disability Savings Bond is a federal government contribution that is received when the beneficiary or the family of a child has a low income. **Personal contributions are not required to receive the Bond.**

Features of the Canada Disability Savings Bond

Features of the Canada Disability Savings Bond include:

- the Canada Disability Savings Bond will provide up to $1,000 per year to an RDSP for an adult whose annual net income is under $24,183 per year

- children under the age of 19 whose family's annual income is under $41,544 per year are also eligible for the $1,000 Bond

- effective in 2011, the Bond will automatically be paid for up to 10 previous years, provided the beneficiary was eligible

- if the adult or family income is between $24,183 and $41,544, then they will be eligible for a Bond of a lesser amount

- the Bond is available to a lifetime total of $20,000

Getting money from an RDSP

Here's what you need to know about withdrawals (often referred to as payments), disability assistance payments, and lifetime disability assistance payments:

- the holder decides when withdrawals are made from the RDSP

- withdrawals can be used for anything (there are no federal or provincial restrictions)

- withdrawals can begin any time (even before age 60!) but remember that a withdrawal made within 10 years of the last federal government contribution will trigger the repayment of the holdback amount

- withdrawals must begin at age 60

- you can make a one time withdrawal (a disability assistance payment) or set up regular payments, monthly or annually (lifetime disability assistance payments)

- when you are ready to set up regular withdrawals, you can use some or all of the RDSP to purchase a life annuity

- if the federal government contributes more than all of your personal contributions, then the total of all withdrawals in any given year will be limited by a formula (approximately the amount in the RDSP divided by the number of years to reach age 83).

For more details on withdrawals visit www.rdsp.com or www.rdspresource.ca.

- a beneficiary may receive both the Grant and the Bond for a lifetime total of $90,000

- a beneficiary can receive the Bond until December 31 of the year in which they turn 49

- no contributions are necessary to receive the Bond.

NOTE If you are eligible for an RDSP you can claim Grants for previous years of eligibility once you start. Effective 2011, entitlements to the Bond will be automatically carried forward for up to 10 years. See New Carry Forward rules on the next page.

Qualifying for the Canada Disability Savings Grant

This chart illustrates how annual RDSP contributions qualify for a matching Grant based on the amount contributed and annual income.

Income (2008)	Contributions (2010)	$$ Amount of Grant	$$ Annual Maximum	$$ Lifetime Maximum
$83,088 or less	First **$500** – contributions into the RDSP	$3 for every $1 contributed	$1,500	$70,000
	Next **$1,000** – personal contributions	$2 for every $1 contributed	$2,000	
More than $83,088	First $1,000	$1 for every $1 contributed	$1,000	$70,000*

*If the annual family income always exceeded the threshold, then the RDSP could not reach the legislated maximum.

Qualifying for the Canada Disability Savings Bond

This chart illustrates that regardless of whether RDSP contributions are made or not, lower income families and adults may qualify for government assistance in the form of a Bond.

Your Income (2008)	Contributions Required	$$ Annual Bond (2010)	$$ Lifetime Maximum
$24,183 or less	$0	$1,000	$20,000
Between $24,183 and $40,970	$0	partial amount based on income	$20,000
Greater than $41,544 (or no income tax return)	$0	$0 – no bond is available	$0

Carry Forward Entitlements

Effective 2011, your relative will be able to get the Grant and Bond amounts for previous years back to 2008, when the RDSP was launched.

CANADA DISABILITY SAVINGS BOND ENTITLEMENTS If your relative is eligible for the Bond for previous years, the federal government will calculate the amount a beneficiary is eligible for and automatically deposit it into their RDSP. Eventually, this will be for up to 10 years. Remember that eligibility is dependent on:

- being a Canadian resident
- eligibility for the Disability Tax Credit
- income as determined from filing income tax for the tax year two years prior to the year in question
- opening the RDSP and applying for the Bond before the end of the year that the beneficiary turns 49.

For example, Pat, a resident of Beaverlodge, Alberta, opened an RDSP in 2011 when she was 35 years old. She has been eligible for the Disability Tax Credit since 2008. She applied for the Bond, has filed her taxes every year, and has had a net income of $14,256 per year since 2006. Based on this information, the federal government will establish her eligibility for the full Bond for the four years 2008 through 2011 and will deposit $4,000 into her RDSP.

CANADA DISABILITY SAVINGS GRANT ENTITLEMENTS If you are just opening an RDSP for your relative or if you haven't made enough contributions in previous years to receive all of the Grant that your relative was eligible to receive, then you can make a contribution and receive the Grant for previous years. The government will utilize Grant entitlements of 3 to 1 before those of 2 to 1 (See the next page for Grant entitlements). Remember that eligibility is dependent on:

- being a Canadian resident
- eligibility for the Disability Tax Credit
- income as determined from filing income tax for the tax year two years prior to the year in question

- opening an RDSP, applying for the Grant, and making contributions before the end of the year that the beneficiary turns 49.

For example, when Pat opened her RDSP, her family made a contribution of $4,000.

Year	3-1 Entitlement	2-1 Entitlement
2008	500	1,000
2009	500	1,000
2010	500	1,000
2011	500	1,000
Total	2,000	4,000

The table above shows Pat's Grant entitlements.

The $4,000 will be first applied to her Grant entitlement as follows:

- 3-1: $2,000 x 3 = $6,000
- 2-1: $2,000 x 2 = $4,000

A total of $10,000 Grant will be deposited to her RDSP. She will have $2,000 in 2-1 entitlements remaining.

Combining the three contributions: Family contribution ($4,000), Grant ($10,000) and Bond ($4,000), Pat will have $18,000 in her RDSP.

RRSP/RRIF Rollover to an RDSP

Effective 2010, new provisions permit parents and grandparents, at death, to rollover RRSPs and RRIFs to the RDSPs of financially dependent children and grandchildren, on a tax-deferred basis.

A person is generally considered to be financially dependent if their income is below a specific threshold ($17,621 for 2010). A person whose income is above this amount may also be considered to be financially dependent if dependency can be demonstrated.

Normally any assets held in RRSPs and RRIFs become income in the year of the death—often leading to a sizeable tax bill. When these assets are passed to the RDSP of a child or grandchild, that tax is waived, leading to sizeable tax savings.

As much as $200,000 can be rolled into an RDSP but the amount of the rollover may not exceed the beneficiary's available RDSP contribution room. This means that if contributions have already been made, then the amount will equal $200,000 minus previous personal contributions.

The rollover will count as contributions towards the beneficiary's lifetime limit but will not be matched by Canada Disability Savings Grants. The rollover will be considered as a personal contribution for the purpose of determining whether personal or government contributions are greater. But because the rollover will not have been subject to income tax, it will be considered taxable when withdrawals are made.

The rollover may be applied to deaths dating back to 2007. Special transition rules apply to deaths occurring before March 4, 2010. If this situation is applicable, we recommend discussing it with your lawyer.

Questions about the RDSP

Why should we open an RDSP if our relative is older?

The RDSP has a couple of advantages no matter how old your relative is. At age 65, people stop receiving AISH and begin receiving Old Age Security and the Guaranteed Income Supplement (GIS). Fifty per cent of taxable income, including income from a trust, is clawed back from GIS. Payments from an RDSP, however, are exempt. Further, the RDSP grows on a tax-deferred basis while income in trusts is taxable.

Therefore, even though your relative is older and they many not receive much, if any, of the Grant or Bond, it is still to their benefit to have an RDSP. It is important to remember that contributions to an RDSP can be made until December 31 of the year in which your relative turns 59.

Can we use an RDSP as a short-term savings plan?

Yes! As indicated above, an RDSP is beneficial when your relative is older. Families who want the flexibility to allow their relatives to use the RDSP right away should forego the Grant and Bond in order to have the freedom to start receiving payments today. If your relative is older, then you don't have the option of saving over many years. In this situation, the RDSP can be used as a short-term savings plan. See Alex's scenario on page 157 for more details.

What happens to my relative's RDSP when they die?

Assets in a person's RDSP become part of the person's estate and are distributed in accordance with their Will. If they don't have a Will, then their assets are distributed according to the *Intestate Succession Act* (Alberta).

If the individual dies within 10 years of receiving any government contributions, then any Grant or Bond received in the previous 10 years must be returned to the government. If 10 years has passed since receiving the last government contributions, then no money needs to be returned.

Who oversees my relative's RDSP?

The person who manages an RDSP is the holder. Parents are the holders when their child is a minor. When their child turns 18, they may continue as the holder, or they can pass the responsibility on to the beneficiary, an adult trustee, or a power of attorney.

NOTE When a plan is opened for a person who is 18 years or older, that person must be the holder of the plan unless they assign that responsibility to their attorney under a Power of Attorney (if they have the capacity to do so) or the Court assigns that responsibility to their trustee under a Trusteeship Order (if they lack the capacity to do so).

PLAN is currently working with the federal government to create a solution so that trusteeship is not the only option available to adults who might not have the ability to manage their own RDSP. For current information, check www.rdsp.com, www.rdspresource.ca, subscribe to your local PLAN affiliate newsletter, or sign up for PLAN's free ezine at www.PLAN.ca.

What you need to do now!

- ensure your relative has a Social Insurance Number
- establish your relative's eligibility for the Disability Tax Credit (see Income Tax Form T2201 or visit www.rdspresource.ca, PLAN's preferred disability tax partner)
- file your Tax Return until your relative is 19 years old
- if your relative is 19 years old, make sure that their Tax Returns have been filed back to the year that they turned 17 or back to the year 2008, whichever date is more recent

- if the beneficiary is a child, make sure you apply for the Canada Child Tax Benefit.

NOTE We estimate that thousands of people in Canada are eligible for the Disability Tax Credit but do not apply because they have no income. Now they have good reason to apply because eligibility for the Disability Tax Credit automatically makes your relative eligible for the Disability Savings Grant and Bond.

Before you buy an RDSP: three questions you might ask your financial institution

RDSPs may vary from one financial institution to another. Make sure your relative's RDSP has the flexibility to meet unforeseen circumstances:

1. Does the RDSP permit Disability Assistance Payments (lump sum payments)?
2. Can the RDSP be transferred to another financial institution without penalty?
3. Are there penalties if you don't meet a contribution schedule?

Tips to get the most out of an RDSP

- start early
- contribute regularly
- maximize Canada Disability Savings Grants
- remember that anyone can contribute to your relative's RDSP
- use PLAN's RDSP calculator to determine your best scenario.

Visit www.plan.ca or www.rdsp.com and click on the RDSP calculator button.

The power of the RDSP

The following scenarios illustrate the potential of the RDSP. We have summarized our assumptions in each situation. Results will vary with different assumptions and your personal circumstances.

The RDSP and young children

Families with young children usually have a list of competing financial priorities. The RDSP represents an economical way for parents, grandparents—and perhaps other family members and friends—to put funds aside for your relative and, and by so doing, have the government contribute as well.

For example, if you have a four year old and are able to put aside $100 a month ($1,200 a year) for 20 years and your family's annual income is below $83,088 (2011 amount), then your child will have over a quarter million dollars when they turn 34. In other words, your investment of $24,000 will multiply over ten times!

HERE'S HOW IT WORKS:

Family taxable income: under $83,088

Son/daughter's income at age 19: under $24,183

Annual family contribution: $1,200 a year

Total family contributions from age 4 to 24: $1,200 times 20 = $24,000

Matching Grant: $58,000

Bond: $6,000 (age 19 to 24)

Total Grant and Bond: $64,000

Investments: moderate risk (estimated return 5.5%)

Value at age 34: $250,000 (approx.)

Annual Lifetime Disability Assistance payments may begin at age 34 without having to repay any of the holdback amount. Unless personal contributions are greater than those of the federal government, then the first payment will be $5,200 and will increase by 5.5% annually. (Remember that it is possible to purchase an annuity with some or all of the capital in the RDSP).

Alternatively, the funds could be withdrawn at a different age. For example:

Value at age 40: $360,000 (approx.)

Value at age 50: $640,000 (approx.)

There are an infinite number of combinations depending on how much you contribute and when. Please visit PLAN's RDSP calculator at www.rdsp.com.

Teens: Natalie

Natalie's squeals of satisfaction when a teammate scores a run are all the reward that her father, Eric, would ever ask for. "She loves being a part of the team and loves the excitement of the competition," says Eric.

While Natalie, like other teens, may be focused on friends and fun, her mother Karin is aware of the uncertainty of the future. "When I close my eyes, I see us on the calm water above Niagara Falls. What's so frightening is that I don't know what comes next."

"The RDSP is a really concrete way to start preparing for the future today. Financial security allows us to shape the future. We can begin to dream with it," adds Eric.

Karin is not currently working outside the home and Eric's annual income is below $83,088; therefore, they will qualify for the maximum annual grant of $3,500.

Karin and Eric think they can put aside $125 a month for an RDSP for a total of $1,500 per year. They plan to contribute for 20 years.

At 47 years of age, Natalie will be able to receive payments without any penalties and the plan will be worth about $350,000. It will pay her about $9,700 a year at the beginning and rise to $48,200 per year when she is 77 years old.

RDSP SUMMARY:

Natalie's age: 17 years

Family taxable income: under $83,088

Natalie's income at age 19: Under $24,183

Annual family contribution: $125 a month ($1,500 a year)

Family contributions from age 17 to 36: $30,000

Value of Grant: $70,000

Value of Bond: $18,000

Investments: moderate risk (estimated return 5.5%)

Age to begin receiving from the plan: 47 years

Approximate value of the RDSP when beginning payments (age 47): $350,000

Annual Lifetime Disability Assistance payments will approximately begin as follows:

$9,700 at age 47

$16,500 at age 57

$28,200 at age 67 and

$48,200 per year at age 77.

Transition to adulthood: Darren

Even in a crowded room Darren seeks out people standing alone, latches onto their arm, and guides them into a conversation. It seems no one can refuse his broad smile.

"It's his gift," says his mom Janice, who keeps a watchful eye on him. "I'm not sure how he will put it to use after he finishes school in June," she sighs.

"I like the idea of the RDSP," she says, "I'm scared to death about the future. But as a single mom, I don't have much left to contribute after I pay the bills every month."

Janice plans to open an RDSP for Darren to get the Canada Disability Savings Bond. She's been to a LACL Will and Estate workshop and has counseled her elderly parents to put the share of their estate they plan to leave for Darren into a discretionary trust (Henson Trust). If he's still young enough, the trust can make contributions to his RDSP. Otherwise, the trust can be used directly to secure his future.

RDSP SUMMARY:

Darren's age: 19 years

Taxable income: under $24,183 (determined by Darren's income)

Annual family contribution: $0

Value of Bond: $20,000

Investments: moderate risk (estimated return 5.5%)

Age to begin receiving from the plan: 49 years

Approximate value of the RDSP when beginning payments (age 49): $60,000

Annual Lifetime Disability Assistance payments will begin at: $1,750 and will rise by about $170 every year.

NOTE The amount in the RDSP could also change if Darren's grandparents contribute to his RDSP.

Young adulthood: Maria

"I'm famous! I'm famous!" shouts Maria, surrounded by the cast of the theatre production of Beauty and the Beast. She glows when she is speaking about musicals, the excitement palpable in her voice. If her parents George and Rosa had enough time (and money), this is where she would spend every evening.

Maria's parents are confident that they can provide a good life for her while they are alive and able. The RDSP provides the means for securing the future when they won't be around.

Rosa and George have a big extended family and, at the last gathering, getting an RDSP started for Maria was a main topic of discussion. The family has set a goal of raising $25,000. George has no doubt it will happen. George and Rosa also plan to contribute $1,500 a year for 20 years.

Maria's age: 27 years

Taxable income: under $24,183 (determined by Maria's income)

Annual family contribution: $125 a month ($1,500 a year)

Total family contributions from age 27 to 46: $55,000 (annual contribution plus $25,000 lump sum amount)

Value of Grant: $70,000

Value of Bond: $20,000

Investments: moderate risk (estimated return 5.5%)

Age to begin receiving from the plan: 57 years

Approximate value of the RDSP when beginning payments (age 57): $475,000.

If an annuity is bought, annual payments will begin at: $24,000 and will rise by an average of about $500 per year. Some or all of the funds in Maria's RDSP could also be used to help purchase a house or to deal with other requirements that may arise.

The future is here: Alex

Tom is a Lifetime Member of PLAN Calgary (the Road Ahead Society). Tom is confident that Alex's future is provided for. His Will is current and he directs his executor to establish a discretionary trust for his son, Alex. Alex also has a Personal Network who will look out for him when Tom passes away.

Alex, who just turned 41, has many interests, including photography and volunteering. His extra time is divided between the local seniors centre and the food bank.

Tom knows that if he capitalizes on the Grant and Bond for the next eight years, Alex won't be able to access the plan until he is 59 years old without paying a penalty. Tom wants him to be able to start using it earlier so he is prepared to forgo the government contribution. What Tom likes is that it will earn income and that Alex can use it for anything he wants without affecting his AISH eligibility and benefits. Tom also knows that—unlike a trust—Alex's RDSP will not affect his Guaranteed Income Supplement, which will replace his AISH benefits once he turns 65.

Tom's plan is to contribute $200,000 as soon as he can and then let it grow for about 10 years.

Tom will still set up a discretionary trust in his Will but the trustee will face more restrictions on spending than the holder of Alex's RDSP. The RDSP and trust combined, however, will provide a good life for Alex.

Tom's plan seems pretty sound. In 10 years, the $200,000 that he contributes will have grown to about $350,000. By purchasing a life annuity that is indexed for inflation at 2%, this will provide Alex with an annual income of about $16,000 per year at age 52, growing to about $29,000 when he is 83 years old, which is pretty good for a $200,000 investment!

RDSP SUMMARY:

Alex's age: 41 years

Taxable income: under $24,183

Family contributions at age 41: $200,000

Value of Grant: $3,500

Value of Bond: $1,000

Investments: moderate risk (estimated return 5.5%)

Age to begin receiving from the plan: 52 years

Approximate value of the RDSP when payments begin (age 52): $350,000.

Comparison – RDSP and Trusts

Appreciating the differences between RDSPs and trusts will help you to determine which option is best for your family member. Some families may want to capitalize on the federal government matching RDSP Grants; others may see trusts as a more viable option. Still, others may want to do both. Please visit www.rdsp.com or speak with your qualified professional advisor for further assistance.

TRUST	RDSP
AGE	
You can establish a discretionary trust for a beneficiary of any age. Non-discretionary trusts can also be established at any age. There are no age restrictions on payments from trusts.	You can establish an RDSP for someone until the end of the year in which they turn 59. The Grant and Bond are only available until the end of the year in which the person turns 49. The younger a person is, the more that person can benefit from the RDSP because: • they have more opportunity to use the matching federal Grant and Bond • the power of compounded income is increased • they can access the funds at a younger age without penalties.
CONTRIBUTION LIMITS	
Although there are no contribution limits on discretionary or non-discretionary trusts, if the non-exempt assets which are held in the trust exceed $100,000, then AISH eligibility and benefits may be affected.	The RDSP has a $200,000 lifetime contribution limit. Combined with the maximum lifetime amount of $70,000 from the Grant and $20,000 from the Bond, the lifetime RDSP contribution maximum is $290,000.

TRUST	RDSP
CONTROL/DIRECTION	
The trustee(s) make decisions about investments and payments from a trust. They have absolute discretion to make these financial decisions if you establish a discretionary trust. Both trustee(s) and alternates can be identified in your Will when you set up the trust. You can also give trustees the power to designate alternates at a later date.	The holder(s) make decisions about investments and payments from an RDSP. Parents or legal guardians must be the holders of an RDSP established for a minor child. Parents can continue in this role once the child becomes an adult. If an RDSP is established for an adult, then the adult must be one of the holders of the RDSP unless there is a Power of Attorney for Property.
INCENTIVES	
Setting up a trust for a relative with a disability is done entirely with private funds. Governments make no contributions nor offer any tax deductions.	The federal government will contribute up to $90,000 through the Grant ($70,000) and Bond ($20,000) to an RDSP.
ELIGIBILITY	
You can set up a trust to benefit anyone with a disability whether they receive AISH benefits or not. However, for a person who is also receiving AISH benefits, the "deemed" benefits from a trust may have an adverse effect on that person's entitlement to receive AISH benefits.	To be able to set up an RDSP, the beneficiary must be: • qualified for the Disability Tax Credit • younger than 60 years • a resident of Canada.
INVESTMENT	
Investment of assets in trusts is limited to prudent investor rules as outlined in the *Trustee Act* unless other investments are permitted in the Will or the trust agreement.	RDSPs are limited to investments that qualify for an RRSP. There are few restrictions.

TRUST	RDSP
LIMITATIONS ON USE OF FUNDS	
Other than the general guidance or direction you give to your trustee(s), there are no limitations on how trustees can use funds from a trust to benefit the beneficiary. There are, however, limitations on how trust funds can be used without adversely affecting eligibility to receive AISH benefits. There are no age restrictions on the use of funds from a trust.	There are no limitations on how funds can be used. If the person receives AISH benefits, then they are free to use funds from AISH for any purpose without affecting their AISH eligibility and benefits. Funds from an RDSP can be used any time but must begin to be paid to the beneficiary at age 60. There are limitations on the amount that can be used from an RDSP if government contributions exceed family contributions.
TAX ON INCOME EARNED	
Trusts must pay taxes on income earned from investments. Income from a trust set up in your Will is taxed at your relative with a disability's marginal tax rate. Income from *inter vivos* trusts are taxed at the highest marginal tax rate. There are some exceptions. Consult with your lawyer for more details.	RDSPs are tax sheltered. Tax is not payable on investments while held by the plan.

TRUST	RDSP
TAX ON PAYMENTS	
Tax may be payable by the beneficiary when funds are spent from the trust.	Tax is payable on the portion of the payments that are made up of government contributions and investment income earned in the RDSP. It is payable in the hands of the beneficiary at their marginal tax rate.
WHAT HAPPENS WHEN THE BENEFICIARY DIES?	
When you set up a trust, you identify who will receive the remaining assets when the beneficiary dies.	When the beneficiary of an RDSP dies, the RDSP becomes part of their estate and is distributed through their Will. If they don't have a Will, distribution is determined by the *Intestate Succession Act* (Alberta).
	NOTE If the individual dies after the 10 year waiting period, the government Grant and Bond do not have to be returned. Some or all of the Grant and Bond must be returned, however, if the person dies before the 10 year period is over.
ROLLOVER FROM AN RRSP OR RRIF	
The federal government has committed to permitting parents and grandparents the ability to rollover funds in an RRSP or RRIF, at death, to a trust for their relative with a disability. There is substantial tax savings in a rollover. The commitment, however, remains outstanding. Check with your lawyer to see if this might be an option for you.	A parent or grandparent can rollover funds in an RRSP or RRIF, at death, to an RDSP. This can result in substantial tax savings.

Worksheet 10 – Will planning

This worksheet will help you clarify your objectives in making a Will. The worksheet is located at the back of this section, on page 168. Take a look at it now. It is based on ones that all lawyers use. You can get a head start by filling out this worksheet in detail. This way, you'll be better prepared for your meeting with your lawyer.

Resources

Consult your local PLAN affiliate, www.plan.ca, or sign up for PLAN's free ezine for information on upcoming seminars about RDSPs and Will and estate planning.

For information on the RDSP, you can visit www.rdsp.com or www.rdspresource.ca, where you will find the best—and most current—information in Canada. You will also find our RDSP Calculator and links to RDSP seminars, such as PLAN's free tele-conference

Looking ahead to retirement

Rod and Christel Makishi recently received an inheritance. With retirement not that far off, they'd now have a cushion for those years ahead. This, they thought, was a good thing until they realized that an inheritance would push them off their disability benefits. Dave Lawson, Executive Director at LACL, used his knowledge of the Registered Disability Savings Plan (RDSP) to help Rod and Christel set up RDSP accounts. Now that the inheritance is inside their RDSPs, it is an exempt asset and therefore, their AISH benefits will stay as is and Rod and Christel will have some financial security in their retirement.

Is your child under the age of 18?

If you have young children and you die without a Will, here's what happens.

ONE Your estate will be divided according to rules outlined on page 126 and summarized as follows:

• the first $40,000 of your property goes to your spouse

• if you die leaving one child, one-half of the remainder of your estate goes to your spouse and one-half goes to your child

• if you die leaving more than one child, one-third of the remainder of your estate goes to your spouse and the remaining two-thirds is divided equally among your children.

• The funds for your children may be held in trust by the Public Trustee of Alberta until they turn 18 **unless** that amount is less than $10,000 and is not payable under a Court Order **or** a trusteeship application is made by the surviving spouse to manage the child's property.

TWO If there is no surviving parent— that is, you both die—or there is no surviving parent who has legal custody, the Public Guardian of Alberta becomes the guardian of their personal care.

To prevent a costly, complicated, and potentially messy and heartbreaking outcome, you must make a Will. If you have children under the age of 18, you must name a legal guardian for those children.

Demystifying definitions that could definitely derail you

AISH Benefits Financial supports in the form of monthly living allowances, health benefits (medical, dental, optical and pharmaceutical) and personal benefits provided to people with disabilities in Alberta.

Beneficiary A person to whom you leave things or who is entitled to receive things through a trust (money, gifts, insurance policy, RRSP). The person who receives funds from an RDSP is also a beneficiary.

Bequest A gift of a specific item of property or a specific amount of cash identified in your Will.

Co-Decision Maker The person appointed by the Court, with the express agreement of an adult suffering from a significant impairment, to assist that adult in making health care or other personal decisions.

Codicil A legal document used to amend portions of your original Will and requiring the same formalities of signing and witnessing needed for a Will.

Discretionary Trust (or Henson Trust) A trust in which the choice as to how to spend the interest and principal is completely in the hands of the trustee.

Enduring Power of Attorney A written document giving someone else the power and authority to conduct and manage your financial affairs even if you become incapable.

Executor (or Personal Representative) The person or professional named in the Will who is responsible for ensuring that the wishes in your Will are carried out.

Grant of Probate A Court Order which is the executor's proof they can act as your executor.

Guardianship The authority to make health and personal care decisions on behalf of another person.

Holder The person who administers an RDSP.

Holdback Amount The amount in an RDSP that must be paid back to the federal government is money is taken out of an RDSP before 10 years after the last government contribution. The holdback is the total amount that the federal government has contributed to the RDSP in the previous 10 years.

Inter Vivos Trust A trust that comes into effect during the lifetime of the person who established the trust. Also known as a Living Trust.

Intestate A person who dies intestate dies without a valid Will.

Life Interest Benefit given to someone in a Will which allows that person to have the use of specific property or a certain sum of money only for the lifetime of that person. The remainder goes to someone else when the person with the life interest dies.

Non-Discretionary Trust A trust in which the beneficiary may have some control over the provisions of the trust, including how to spend the principal and interest.

Non-Probatable Assets Assets that pass outside of the Will. For example, joint tenant ownership of real estate and bank accounts, RRSP/RRIF, life insurance, and annuities if beneficiaries have been designated.

Personal Directive A written document giving someone else the authority to make personal care decisions on your behalf should you not have the capacity to do so.

Probate The procedure by which the Will of the deceased person is legally approved by the court and documented. It also confirms the appointment of your Executor.

Revocation Cancelling parts of or all of an existing Will.

Settlor The individual who establishes a trust.

Specific Decision-Maker The person appointed under the *Adult Guardianship and Trustee Act* to give or refuse treatment on behalf of another person when a Personal Directive or guardianship order does not exist.

Substitute Decision-Maker The person authorized by the *Adult Guardianship and Trustee Act* to seek permission for health care when a Personal Directive or Guardianship Order does not exist.

Supported Decision Maker The person appointed by an adult with capacity to help that adult make health care and other decisions of a personal nature.

Testator The person who makes the Will.

Testamentary Trust A trust set up in a Will that only takes effect after your death.

Trust A legal arrangement in which one person (the Settlor) transfers legal title in certain property to a trustee to manage the property for the benefit of a person (the beneficiary).

Trustee The person or company that manages the trust according to the instructions in the trust agreement or Will.

Worksheet 10

Will planning

This worksheet is intended to:

- assist you in compiling information to take to your lawyer when you wish to make your Will
- assist in making you aware of decisions you will need to make and to help you make them.

After completing the worksheet you will be ready to contact a lawyer of your choice to make the Will. This worksheet does not give any legal advice. To draft a Will, you need to see a qualified lawyer.

A. Personal and Family Particulars

Date _____

1 Full Name _____

Address _____

Occupation _____

Home Phone _____ Office Phone _____

Date of Birth_____ Place of Birth _____

Citizenship _____

Marital Status (including plans to marry) _____

Date of Marriage_____ Place of Marriage _____

Do you have a marriage contract? _____

Have you or your spouse been married or lived in a common law relationship before?_____

2   Marriage or Common Law Relationship _____

Spouse's Full Name _____

Address _____

Occupation _____

Home Phone _____   Office Phone _____

Date of Birth_____   Place of Birth _____

Citizenship _____

3   Children (Please list all children of either spouse. Please note with a * any child of a former
    marriage of either spouse and with ** any child with a disability. Please include children you
    have adopted and children of any previous marriages or common law relationships.)

Full Name   Date of Birth

_____   _____

_____   _____

_____   _____

_____   _____

4 Other Dependents

Is there someone who is dependent upon you for financial support for whom you wish to provide, such as an elderly parent? _____

If yes, please complete the following:

Full Name _____

Address _____

Relationship _____

5 Other Responsibilities

Are you now serving as the legal guardian or trustee for an adult who has a disability or lacks capacity? _____

If yes, full name, address and relationship to you:

Full Name _____

Address _____

Relationship _____

Relationship to you _____

B. Will Particulars

1 Appointment of Guardian(s) for Infant Children

Do you have a child under the age of 18?

> **It is important to note that you CANNOT appoint a guardian for your child with a disability who is older than 18.**

Who will be their guardian(s) should you die before they reach age 18?

Name	Address	Relationship to you	Occupation

Who will be their alternate guardian(s) before they reach age 18?

Name	Address	Relationship to you	Occupation

2   Distribution of Your Estate

(a) Do you wish to leave your estate to your spouse if he/she survives you? _____

(b) Do you wish to share your estate between your spouse and your children? _____

 If so, how? _____

(c) If your spouse dies before you, do you wish to leave your estate to your children? _____

If so, in equal shares? _____

If in unequal shares, what proportion or amount is each child to get?_____

_____

(d) At what age do you wish your children to receive their share?_____

(e) If any child fails to survive to that age, do you wish his or her children to receive the share?

_____

(f) If one of your children dies before you do, who do you wish to receive his or her share of your estate?_____

(g) If your spouse and children all die before you do, who do you want to receive

your estate?_____

3 Establishing a trust for someone receiving AISH benefits

(a) Do you have a relative who is in receipt (or likely in the future to be in receipt) of AISH benefits? ☐ Yes ☐ No

(b) Do you wish to set up a trust for this relative? ☐ Yes ☐ No

(c) Do you wish it to be a discretionary trust? ☐ Yes ☐ No

(d) Who do you wish to be trustees of this trust?

Name	Address	Relationship to you	Occupation

NOTE You may have any number of co-trustees. You should discuss with your lawyer whether you want each trustee to be a co-trustee or an alternate trustee. You should also discuss with your lawyer the ability of your named trustees to appoint additional or successor trustees.

(e) Who do you wish to be alternate trustees if any of the ones you have named are unable to serve?

Name	Address	Relationship to you	Occupation

(f) Residual Beneficiary

When you set up a trust you must specify what happens to the assets left in the trust when the person whom the trust was set up for dies.

Who do you want to receive the assets left in the trust when the person for whom the trust was set up for dies?_____

Does this cause a conflict of interest? _____
You should make sure you discuss a potential conflict of interest with your lawyer.

(g) Trustee Powers

Do you wish your trustee to be able, if it becomes necessary or desirable, to buy, sell, rent, lease, or mortgage a residence for your relative with a disability?_____

If so, make sure you discuss your wishes with your lawyer. They will need to ensure they give the powers you want to your trustees.

Do you wish to give your trustees unrestricted investment powers to allow them to make any investment they think is appropriate? _____

     Or

Do you wish them to be restricted in what they can invest? _____

It is important to discuss with your lawyer the powers you wish to give to your trustees.

Do you want to leave a particular asset to a particular person? This includes clothing, jewelry, art, etc. If so, describe below. _____

_____

_____

Do you want to give a cash gift to anyone? If so, describe below.

_____

_____

_____

Do you want to give cash or another gift to charity? If so, describe below.

_____

_____

_____

You must be aware that some assets can pass outside of your Will.

Have you filed a beneficiary designation with the plan issuers for your:

a) RRSP ☐ Yes ☐ No

b) RRIF ☐ Yes ☐ No

c) Pension Plan ☐ Yes ☐ No

d) Life Insurance Policy ☐ Yes ☐ No

If so, these items will pass outside of your Will.

Do you own any other assets, for example property, bank accounts, etc. jointly with another person? ☐ Yes ☐ No

If so, these items will pass outside of your Will.

4   Additional Support for your relative

Do you wish PLAN to provide support for your relative when you are no longer able to do so? If so, contact PLAN to discuss incorporating appropriate clauses into your Will that will enable PLAN to assist your relative.

5   Other Comments or Instructions

_____

_____

_____

This is for additional information, which your lawyer might need to consider.

_____

_____

_____

C. Asset and Debt Summary

(please indicate if these assets or debts are not in Alberta)

	Hers	His	Both
a) Cash and Term Deposits	$_____	$_____	$_____

b) Life Insurance

Insurance Co	Owner of Policy	Designated Beneficiary	Amount
_____	_____	_____	$_____
_____	_____	_____	$_____
_____	_____	_____	$_____

c) RRSPs

RRSP Institution	Owner of RRSP	Designated Beneficiary	Amount
_____	_____	_____	$_____
_____	_____	_____	$_____
_____	_____	_____	$_____

	Her name	His name	Joint Names
d) Stocks and Bonds	$_____	$_____	$_____
e) Pension Plans & Annuities	$_____	$_____	$_____

f) Describe any interests you may have in any proprietorships, partnerships or private companies. _____

g) Real Estate

	No.1	No.2
Address	_____	_____
Registered Owner(s)	_____	_____
Joint Tenants?	_____	_____
Estimated Value	$_____	$_____
Mortgage Balance (estimated)	$_____	$_____
Mortgage Life Insured?	☐ Yes ☐ No	☐ Yes ☐ No
Approximate equity	$_____	$_____

h) Personal Effects

Approximate value of household goods, furniture, jewelry, boats & automobiles: $_____

Are any of these articles owned jointly with someone else? ☐ Yes ☐ No

i) Miscellaneous

A) Interest in any existing estate or trusts: _____

B) Other substantial assets: _____

C) Do you have any real or personal property outside of Alberta? If so, please specify.

_____

D. Summary of Debts (other than mortgages previously noted)

Creditor	Life Insurance	Amount
_____	☐ Yes ☐ No	$_____
_____	☐ Yes ☐ No	$_____
_____	☐ Yes ☐ No	$_____

Estimated Net Value of Estate

	Her name	His name	Joint Names
Total Assets	_____	_____	_____
Less Total Debts	_____	_____	_____
Less Estimated Tax	_____	_____	_____
Liability	_____	_____	_____
Total Net Value of Estate	$_____	$_____	$_____

securing your plan

Before my stroke, I had a mistaken notion that feminism meant independence; the unspoken corollary was that disability (and aging) meant shameful dependence on others.

What I have learned finally is that in asking for help I offer other people an opportunity for intimacy and collaboration. Whether I am asking for me personally or for disabled people generally, I give them the opportunity to be their most human.

In Judaism, we call this gift a mitzvah.

BONNIE SHERR KLEIN

Maggie the teacher

The lesson of a good life

MY DAUGHTER MAGGIE and so many others enjoy their good lives, thanks to the hard work of the families who created the Lethbridge Association for Community Living and similar groups across Alberta.

Fifty years previously, these pioneer families worked hard to make a better world for their sons and daughters… a world where people with developmental disabilities would not be cut off from their families or excluded from having opportunities to live a good life.

These families also worked hard to keep their kids at home and to bring others out of the institutions.

And when the education system said their kids were uneducable, parents, families and friends worked hard to enable kids to go to school.

First they created the Dorothy Gooder School in Lethbridge, but after some years, they worked just as hard to close that school so all kids could go to the same neighborhood schools as their sisters and brothers and friends.

There is still work to be done. Some people still live in isolated institutions instead of in their home communities. Inclusive education is still challenging. Employment is sometimes treated more as charity than as meaningful work. Relationships and friendships are often at risk, especially when moms and dads near the ends of their lives.

Our Association has accomplished much over these past 50 years. As long as inequality and discrimination remain, we will continue to be inspired by their example and pledge to leave a new generation of families with the same positive legacy we received. ∎

Securing your plan

Achieving a good life and a secure future for your relative requires careful attention to a number of key elements:

- a vision with as much detail as you, your relative, and close family and friends can muster
- the ongoing involvement of caring, committed friends and family
- control over the home environment
- trusted friends and family to assist with decision-making
- a properly drawn and executed Will
- a financial strategy including an RDSP and a discretionary trust
- sensitive and caring trustees who know your family member.

We trust you've also thought about:

- how you want to divide your property and financial assets
- which relative, friend, Personal Network member, or company might be a trustee or co-trustee of the discretionary trust
- what services you may want from a lawyer, accountant, trust officer, and financial planner
- consolidating all this valuable information in the worksheets provided throughout this book!

We trust you now have a clear idea about what your relative's life will look like after you are gone. Your picture includes:

- who their friends will be
- where they might live
- how they will make their contribution to society
- what might be put in place to keep them safe
- who might serve as an advocate and monitor
- what role your other family members might play.

Even small steps away from segregation lead to a better life, when taken with conviction and respect.

MARILYN DOLMAGE

Worksheet 11—Your Summary Checklist—can be found at the end of this step, on page 202.

Yes, purple

KARIN IS THE YOUNGEST of four children. She has seen her siblings graduate and move away for post-secondary education, get jobs, and marry. So it was no surprise when Karin told her high school teacher that her goals were to graduate from grade 12, go to college, get a job, get a boyfriend, get married, and move to a purple house. Of course.

With that kind of clarity we began to plan... three years earlier than we anticipated thanks to the advice of a wise high school teacher.

Planning is a combination of being deliberate while being open to what emerges. Like the time Karin invited Christina, a work experience student to her birthday party. I saw first hand how naturally she interacted with everyone. As chance would have it, Christina—who was taking time off before going on to university to become a special needs teacher—was looking for work. I offered her a job on the spot. I had no idea if I could sell this to PDD but I was determined.

A top priority was for Karin to learn the local transit system so Karin and Christina went off to Calgary Transit's transit training program.

Karin learned to always stand by a help button on the platform and to always pay attention to where the help button is on the train. Recently, they were on a train when a medical emergency occurred and Karin was able to see first hand how the help button was used.

The relationship between Karin and Christina is undeniably very special. They even plan to be bridesmaids for each other.

I used my Air Miles to arrange for the two of them to go to Disneyland. They had a blast, egging each other on and just having fun. Without a doubt, Christina is a gift.

Karin has completed high school and proudly walked across the stage at her graduation. She now attends classes at Mount Royal University, has had jobs at Toys R Us and Gap, and is still looking for a boyfriend.

It looks likely that Karin will begin looking for her own place when she turns 25.

And just in case we forget, Karin points out purple houses whenever she sees them!

VAL AND KARIN HAZLE

Families helping families

Your challenge is to make the necessary arrangements for your relative to have a safe, secure, and comfortable life beyond your lifetime. This is an immense challenge. Who knows what the future will be like? They haven't yet invented a cell phone that works from the grave but if they do, the inventor will be a parent of a child with a disability! In the meantime, who can you count on?

If you are like us, you may still have one nagging concern: Who does what I do, keeping an eye on everything? Who will be my eyes and ears, my arms and legs? Who will monitor the plans I have made? What is my plan "B"?

Our answer is simple: trust other families in similar circumstances. PLAN was created so we could share our strength, expertise, and know-how. PLAN was created by a small group of families who wanted a new type of organization: one controlled by families, one that would remain financially independent, and one that would focus exclusively on the social and financial well-being of our relatives with disabilities.

PLAN offers four basic functions which correspond to the four letters in our name:

PLANNING FOR THE FUTURE PLAN offers current information on everything you will need to plan for the future (and deal with the present for that matter). This includes information on:

- the Registered Disability Savings Plan (RDSP)
- Wills and estates
- trusts
- government benefits
- home ownership
- disability tax benefits
- creating a social network.

LIFETIME MEMBERSHIP We offer this for families who want PLAN as a back up to monitor all the plans they have put in place and to intervene and advocate where necessary.

> I knew I loved him, and he knew I knew it. I held that sweetness in my arms, and waited for whatever was going to happen next. We did that together.
>
> IAN BROWN

Pen pals for life: Bethany and Julia

MY NAME IS BETHANY and I live in a pink house called Little Flower on 6 Sandpiper Court in Sherwood Park, Alberta. My house is a L'Arche home. I have three roommates: Henry, Robin and Tim.

PLAN asked if we'd share some of our letters. This is my letter about my life. My mom's letter comes next.

When I was a girl, my Mom and Dad had to move away for work. They didn't want me living in hotels. So I took some holidays to try L'Arche. I like where I live and it smells like food cooking.

Mom and Dad live way up north and I wanted to live with them but I would have had to live in a hotel too much. I am happy where I live now but still would love to live with Mom and Dad. I love the way she cooks fish and chips. I have two brothers, one in Calgary and one in Mexico. I go to church with Tom and Alana.

I work at the WOW cake factory making boxes and putting stickers on. I have four friends there. I had some special friends from St. Patrick's School too and people I have met through PLAN. My job I have through the Robin Hood Association. I work four days a week, for four and a half hours a day.

These are some things I don't like: fatty food, and hip-hop dance because it hurts my feet.

My dream is to go to Disneyland and see Peter Pan fly.

I miss Mom and Dad but I get very excited when they come.

Bethany

Dear Bethany,

Thank you so much for your letter. It is very good for me to know what you think and how you feel in your heart.

When your Dad and I had to move to Yellowknife to work, we all enjoyed living together in a nice big house. You did indeed make some very special friends at St. Patrick's High School. I remember Sister Nancy, Sonia and Terri just for a start. You were also a good athlete, active in Special Olympics bowling, swimming, skating and skiing. The first year you lived in Yellowknife you won a trophy as Female Athlete of the Year. We were all so proud!

After you graduated from St. Pat's, you wanted to go back to Edmonton, so we had to find you a good and safe place to live. Hotels are great, but as you said, they are not HOME. Before your home in L'Arche was ready, Tom and Alana invited you to live with them in Sherwood Park. That was great, and you love them to this day, I know.

continued on next page

Pen pals...

It made me feel very loved by you when you wrote that you would still like to live with your Dad and me. But I know that from the very first visit, when you "tried" L'Arche, you would have a very interesting and full life within the L'Arche community. We can still visit back and forth and take trips together, as we have been doing, and we will cook all your favourite foods. Maybe someday we will even get to Disneyland and see that flier Peter Pan!

You know, I don't like fatty foods either. They taste good but are not healthy. Your friends in L'Arche have told me recently that you are looking good these days, especially in your new clothes. I am sorry to hear that dancing hurts your feet… you were always my favourite dancing partner! But I know that you still enjoy bike riding, which is very good exercise.

We are very proud of you now too, my girl, knowing that you have an important job at WOW Factor, work which brings you fun and friendship and the sense of a job well-done. You make pretty good money, too!

I love to visit at WOW and also at Robin Hood Association, especially when I can share your coffee breaks.

Gotta run now, but I will write you again soon.

> *Love and prayers forever, Mom*

ADVOCACY We offer both personal advocacy for individuals and families and public policy advocacy to improve the lives of all people with disabilities.

NETWORK We help you create and maintain a Personal Network for your family member.

Flowers and compost

When you think of it, our job description is much like a gardener's: to nurture, to hover, to be alert to changing conditions, to provide shelter from the storm, to fertilize where appropriate, to enjoy all stages of growth, to savour the beauty of the moment, and to appreciate the sweat of preparation. You learn a lot about life as a gardener. You learn, for instance, about the interrelationship between flowers and compost.

A beautiful rose that we have just cut and placed in our vase is very pure. It smells good, fresh, and fragrant. Rotting compost is the opposite.

But that is only if we look on the surface. If we look more closely, we will see that in five or six days the rose will become part of the compost. The truth is, we do not need to wait that long. We can see it now. Take a deep look at the rose. Can you see the compost in the rose? Take another look at the compost. Can you see the rose in the compost?

If you are a gardener, you recognize that you cannot have one without the other. The rose and the compost are equal. The compost is just as precious as the rose.

If you are a parent, you understand that much of the beauty you create arises out of life's darker moments or in response to threats on the horizon. It is also true for us as a movement of families.

The parent-based disability movement arose at the end of the Second World War in the wake of the eugenics movement and the atrocities committed against people with disabilities. It also arose in reaction to professional advice to send our children away to institutions. Those early seeds of change, planted in dank soil, have blossomed into the most wondrous of plants.

The parent-based disability movement was the first internationally-based consumer movement. It led to the creation of the UN Charter of Human Rights for Persons with Disabilities. Before Ralph Nader, before consumerism, we existed!

Looking into the future

We see some disturbing trends and new challenges on the horizon which we are paying close attention to. Think of these challenges as the weather conditions that any sensible gardener needs to prepare for. So let's descend underground into the compost and poke around for a while. Perhaps we'll see the seeds of a solution, the beginning of another beautiful plant!

CHANGING DEMOGRAPHICS Within 15 years, population aging will be a key challenge facing our national and provincial economies. The aging of society and increasing health costs are two other challenges.

The potential impact is threefold. One, there will be fewer taxpayers and therefore smaller operating budgets at every level of government.

Two, health care costs are much higher in the last few years of life. Demographic change reflected in the increase in the elderly dependency ratio is the main factor expected to drive public health care costs.

Three, with a smaller fiscal pie and a greater share of the smaller pie going to health costs, there will be fewer resources to respond to social, educational, and environmental challenges.

Not everyone agrees on the size of the fiscal challenge we face. Every expert has a different set of assumptions. Maybe health care costs won't rise as dramatically as predicted. Maybe a new wave of immigration will fuel our economy. Maybe our birth rate will stop declining. We can't predict how governments will respond and how successful they will be in reining in health costs, and creating more efficiencies.

There is something bigger than fact: the underlying spirit, all it stands for, the mood, the vastness, the wildness.

EMILY CARR

> No amount
> of thought
> can ever reveal
> what comes
> unexpectedly.
>
> ARTHUR ERICKSON

We do think it is prudent, however, to recognize there may be less financial resources to spend on disability supports in the future.

NEW WORTHINESS DEBATE Relatives, friends, and supporters of vulnerable people are constantly reminded of how fragile society's support for people with disabilities can be. Debates about mercy killing, right to die legislation, and a reverence for technology and genetic engineering reflect a quest for perfection and implicitly a belief that some lives are not worth living. With every new tragedy or scientific discovery, fears surface that ambiguous terms like "quality of life" will be used within an emerging "new" eugenics movement. In the past, funding shortfalls have been linked to cutbacks in support for people deemed not as worthy; that is, because they are not contributors or productive and, therefore, are a drain on society's limited resources. Our challenge is to ensure our relatives with disabilities will have fair access to future medical treatment and other government funded supports.

New solutions for changing times

Fortunately families are used to turning adversity around. Reduced tax bases and the increasing size of health care budgets are just the latest in a series of challenges we have faced before. We are confident the natural ingenuity and creativity of families will lead to new solutions for our changing times. PLAN is one of them.

PLAN Affiliates—part of an international movement

PLAN Calgary (www.plancalgary.ca)

PLAN Calgary (formerly known as The Road Ahead Society of Calgary) is a family organization committed to supporting persons with disabilities as they develop meaningful relationships in the community, build positive lives, and create their vision for a sustainable future.

PLAN Calgary will provide assistance in establishing and maintaining a Personal Network.

PLAN Calgary also supports families by holding workshops and information sessions including Beyond Graduation, Planning for a

Good Life, A Home of One's Own, the Registered Disability Savings Plan, and Wills and Estate Planning. PLAN Calgary also presents to other organizations and parent support groups, and participates in resource fairs within its community.

PLAN Calgary has a licence to develop Tyze Microsites for each of its Lifetime Members. The decision of whether or not to develop a Microsite is up to each family. The Tyze system encourages collaboration and networking, just like Facebook. However, it differs because it is secure, free of advertisements, and because people can participate only when invited: no outside lurkers are allowed in.

PLAN Edmonton (www.planedmonton.ca)

The core mission of Plan Edmonton is to assist families to plan for the future of their relative with a disability. It is a family directed organization that supports families through future planning consultations, information sessions, and the development of a Personal Network for their family member.

A Personal Network is central to the services PLAN Edmonton provides. A PLAN Edmonton facilitator is contracted to organize and facilitate the development of a circle of support. The PLAN Edmonton facilitator assists in identifying the goals and dreams of the individual with a disability and in securing the participation and commitment of members of the network. PLAN Edmonton monitors, supports, and maintains the network and invites new members as required.

PLAN Edmonton is structured to ensure it will always be directed by and accountable to families.

PLAN Edmonton supports families through future planning consultations, information sessions, and the development of a social supportive network for their family member.

Lethbridge Association for Community Living (www.lacl.ca)

LACL's vision is that every person can live and participate in the community lifelong. LACL works to ensure that people with disabilities are included as full citizens in their communities. In that regard, they work diligently in partnership with community to ensure that children and adults with disabilities fully benefit from all the systems—such as

> Because Bill is so open about his needs and feelings I found I could talk about my own, something I feel society has discouraged men to do.
>
> DOUG, A PERSONAL NETWORK MEMBER

schools, employers and government programs. LACL staff or an expert family volunteer can provide advocacy services to:

- empower families through information and education
- accompany you to meetings with schools, service providers, or government departments
- connect you with other families with similar experiences
- write letters
- hold meetings
- organize public events
- work with media
- do whatever they can to raise awareness and create change.

LACL will work with families to establish and maintain Personal Networks. They will support families in the facilitation and development of a strong meaningful future plan that is built on the hopes and dreams of the focus person.

> A social enterprise fulfills its mission by earning its income. It also sits on untapped resources which can be mobilized for social good.

Planned Lifetime Advocacy Network (PLAN)

The families who created PLAN had a clear list of do's and don'ts. Do create an organization that can withstand the winds of change. Don't rely on government funding. Do become financially self-sufficient. Don't do anything to weaken your effectiveness as advocates and monitors.

These families wanted an organization that would:

- survive them
- not drift from its mission in a search for funding
- keep an independent eye on all the plans they had made for their individual relatives as well as for all persons with disabilities.

While each Alberta affiliate organization operates independently, together they share the core values, concepts, and approaches that embody the PLAN model.

PLAN's core values

Our founding parents lived through decades of changes affecting their relatives. Many of them created the original parent-led community living and disability organizations. They had experienced the ups and downs of government funding. They knew the quality of programs and services could vary. They knew what to avoid and what to emphasize. They wanted to create a positive organization based on a spirit of abundance. They built our organization around four core values:

1. relationships keep people safe and are the foundation of a good life
2. financial self-sufficiency—no reliance on government funding for organizational operating costs
3. family leadership—our constitution calls for a majority of board members to be family members
4. contributing citizenship—the contributions of our relatives leads to their recognition as full citizens and brings meaning to their lives.

PLAN's four basic functions

FUTURE PLANNING ADVISORY SERVICE

PLAN offers up-to-date information on all the elements of future planning.

CREATING AND MAINTAINING A PERSONAL NETWORK

PLAN believes the best time to consolidate friends and family into a Personal Network of support is NOW. PLAN's future involvement in the life of a person with a disability is conditional upon the existence of a Personal Network and PLAN's active involvement with the individual, the Personal Network, and the family. Without this personal and intimate contact with people and their families, PLAN would not be in a position to understand—let alone advocate for—the best interests of the person with a disability.

FAMILY SUPPORT AND ADVOCACY

A common response from families associated with PLAN is the degree of support and comfort they derive from working together. Families with Personal Networks meet regularly to share concerns and to seek advice from each other. Families accompany each other to critical meetings as advocates.

On a broader scale, PLAN works closely with provincial and federal governments to advocate for legal and financial improvements that will benefit people with disabilities.

LIFETIME COMMITMENT

This is the ultimate and most fundamental function of PLAN. Families can take advantage of all the services offered by PLAN. However, if you want PLAN to watch over and protect the best interests of your relative after you die, then you must become a lifetime member.

PLAN: a social enterprise

Since our founding parents did not want us to rely on government funding, we became a social enterprise. A social enterprise is a new type of not-for-profit organization that fulfills its social mission by earning its income. Social enterprises realize they sit on untapped resources which can be mobilized for social good.

Our expertise was detailed knowledge about what parents and families needed in order to create a safe and secure future for their relatives. This brought us in touch with credit unions, banks, life insurance companies, law firms, and financial and estate planning advisors who were interested in catering to this emerging segment of the disability market.

PLAN's social audit: staying faithful to our values

Our social audit measures member satisfaction and our effectiveness at achieving our goals. It gathers input from our individual and family members, Personal Networks, staff, business partners, and community supporters.

If you would like to read what families have to say about PLAN check out www.plan.ca or www.socialaudit.ca.

Our social enterprise revenue sources include:

- partnering with law firms, financial institutions, and companies who are in the future planning business
- charging a fee for our products and services.

Our emergence as a social enterprise has not been without struggle. It was a difficult decision to charge for our services. But we knew without financial independence our effectiveness as advocates was limited. We now have an Endowment Fund to assist those who cannot afford to pay our nominal fees.

There are many benefits to being a social enterprise. It has enabled us to stay faithful to our core values. We are able to use our new found economic muscle to further our social objectives. Our diverse funding base has made us more stable financially. The money we earn doesn't come with strings attached. This flexibility enables us to respond to emerging needs such as, for example, launching the campaign to create the RDSP.

Perhaps more importantly, being a social enterprise allows us to earn our own way. We are confident this independent economic base prepares us for whatever the future holds and is a model for other organizations to follow.

The emerging disability market

Most of us have heard about the green economy—businesses dedicated to reducing pollution and lightening our ecological footprint. Perhaps you have heard of the grey dollar, that is, products and services purchased by seniors. Or pink tourism—businesses catering to travel by gays and lesbians. These are all markets that have grabbed the attention of businesses and companies.

As we developed and matured as a social enterprise we discovered there was also a disability market. One of the most promising areas for the future of the disability sector is to mobilize this market to assist with our financial sustainability. For example, the estimated RDSP market in Canada is at least $80 billion. The trust market size is another $80 billion. $160 billion is a lot of money! Can you think of ways we can

If you are interested in learning more about social enterprise and social finance, please visit www. planinstitute.ca and click on Innovate with Us.

mobilize our collective economic wealth to protect the future of people with disabilities?

We can.

Some of our ideas include pooling the capital in our RDSPs and trusts to create a Disability Investment Fund. Another idea is to establish a No One Alone Fund to finance the costs of social networks. We are convinced that harnessing our collective economic power is a critical component in securing the future for all people with disabilities. Contact PLAN if you are interested in pursuing any of these initiatives.

Linking with families throughout Canada and around the world

AL ETMANSKI

Al writes regularly about disability, social innovation, solution-based advocacy, inspiration, and solving tough problems. Keep current with Al's thinking and activities by subscribing to his popular blog www.aletmanski.com.

APPARTENANCE-BELONGING

Appartenance-Belonging is about the living ties that connect us to each other, our families, our communities, our country, our beliefs, our earth, and our universe. It is about all forms of life. It is a website that explores our universal desire to belong—to be a part of something grander than ourselves.

Appartenance-Belonging emerged from the bonds of friendship and respect three groups of people—L'Agora, L'Arche, and the PLAN institute for Caring Citizenship—have for each other.

This group shines a light on this mysterious, elusive, majestic, and essential life force, and sees this as the pre-condition for a revolution of belonging.

Appartenance/Belonging is not your usual website. It has evolved slowly, sifting through the insights and wisdom of friends. It owes a spiritual and intellectual debt to Jean Vanier the founder of L'Arche and to Jacques Dufresne the founder of L'Agora encyclopedia and website. It remains a labour of love. Please visit www.appartenance-belonging.org.

> Adopting the right attitude can convert a negative stress into a positive one.
>
> HANS SELYE

PHILIA DIALOGUE ON CARING CITIZENSHIP

When we think of citizenship, we usually think of rights and responsibilities. There is an expectation that everyone in society has a responsibility to contribute. Our friends and family members want to contribute. They are an under-utilized resource in society. We believe the next advance for people with disabilities will be made from this theoretical foundation. To promote these ideas, we created an international web dialogue on caring citizenship and called it Philia, which means neighbourly love. Please visit www.philia.ca.

PLAN INSTITUTE FOR CARING CITIZENSHIP

To respond to the growing interest in PLAN from across Canada and around the world, we created the PLAN Institute.

The PLAN Institute:

- provides on-line courses, workshops, training, and consultation on caring citizenship; social network facilitation; social enterprise; family leadership; organizational development; and social innovation
- mentors groups of families who are adapting the PLAN model
- distributes books, CD ROM's, and DVD's
- researches and publishes on citizenship, social networks, and belonging.

The Institute currently supports over 40 replications around the world. It offers an annual Leadership Training course for people interested in learning about the PLAN model. For those interested in learning about social movements, the Institute offers a four day retreat called *Thinking Like a Movement*. For more information about the PLAN Institute visit www.planinstitute.ca.

SOCIAL INNOVATION GENERATION (SiG)

SiG seeks to address Canada's social and ecological challenges by creating a culture of continuous social innovation. Its focus is on social innovation with particular attention paid to innovations that engage vulnerable and excluded people, that encourage and benefit from the abundant natural, social, and cultural diversity of Canada and its rich heritage of innovation. Al Etmanski and PLAN Institute are founding partners of SiG. Please visit www.sigeneration.ca.

PLAN: A MODEL FOR CREATIVE PROBLEM-SOLVING BY FAMILIES

PLAN is an organization providing hands on, practical support to families and people with disabilities. It is also a movement of families. In the broadest sense, PLAN is about:

- strengthening the family arm of the disability movement
- working together on behalf of all our family members with disabilities
- welcoming supporters from all sectors of society
- focusing on the abilities of ourselves, our relatives, and our neighbours
- seeing the possibilities by creating a climate of continuous innovation
- meeting government as an equal
- putting all our eggs in one basket and treating them gently
- finding roses in the compost.

We were struck recently by a comment from one of our founding members, Joan. She pioneered the development of services and programs for many people with disabilities and has been a long time advocate for families. "I'm having so much fun," she said. "It reminds me of the early days of the parent movement. Everything is so positive. Rather than tearing down, we are constructing something new. It so much easier to get things done. So much more satisfying."

Achieving the complete Personal Future Plan

This book presents six steps for preparing for the future—and indeed changing the present—for your relative:

STEP ONE – CLARIFYING YOUR VISION

Rallying people around your hopes for the future.

STEP TWO – NURTURING FRIENDSHIP

Creating and maintaining a strong network of caring, committed friends and supporters.

STEP THREE – CREATING A HOME

Making a house a home.

STEP FOUR – MAKING SOUND DECISIONS

Protecting vulnerabilities and honouring choices.

STEP FIVE – ACHIEVING FINANCIAL SECURITY

Wills, trusts, and the RDSP: Using all the legal and financial tools at your disposal.

STEP SIX – SECURING YOUR PLAN

Appointing and mentoring your replacements whether they are individuals or organizations like PLAN.

As you have seen, each step builds on the last one. Each one on its own advances the opportunity for greater safety and a better life. The steps are also interrelated and, taken together, they offer a complete system of checks and balances. They may not be foolproof but they are thorough. And that's what is needed to replace what families do now and to provide continuity from one generation to the next.

No one, not even those who have been involved in the future planning business for decades, is ever satisfied with their final product. There will always be tinkering and adjusting. That's natural. The difference is you will be amending a plan that is already in place. The hard work will already have been done and the basics will have been covered.

We can assure you the results will lead to peace of mind.

Conclusion

Safe and Secure is a book for gardeners. We have supplied you with the seeds of inspiration and information. But it is up to you to supply the rest—the planting, the weeding, the watering, and the nurturing. We are confident your shovel and hoe will dig a path into new territory. You will make the rows boldly and follow them fearfully. You will go where the rows lead. At the end you will have created your garden. In your hands your garden will have flourished. It will have become a place of security and repose.

We have supplied the seeds. You supply the love.

In concluding this book we wanted to end with a final story that would motivate or inspire you to march right out and do everything that needs to be done. The truth is, we've already written everything we know. We've nothing left to say. No final flourish. We're still in the field ourselves, you see. Look around you. There we are, your companion gardeners.

Worksheet 11

Your summary checklist

I have completed all the following documents:

☐ A family portrait of my relative.

☐ My letter to the future, clarifying my wishes.

☐ A list of my relative's documents: birth certificate, social insurance card, health care card, etc.

☐ An up-to-date Will that reflects my current wishes.

☐ A description of the purpose of the trust.

☐ An up-to-date list of my major assets and where they are kept (insurance policies, bank accounts, stocks, mutual funds, and so on).

and

☐ I have stored all these documents in a safe place.

☐ My executor knows where these documents are kept.

RESOURCES

Reading List

Becoming Human
Jean Vanier
House of Anansi Press Limited, 1998
We could have chosen any number of Jean Vanier's books because they are all worth reading. This book is illustrative of the power of Jean's insight which is inspired by people with disabilities.

The Body Silent
Robert F. Murphy
New York: W. W. Norton, 1990
Without a doubt this is one of the best books written about and by people with disabilities. An anthropologist writes about his own gradual experience of becoming a person with a disability and what keeps him safe and maintains his quality of life.

Breaking Bread and Nourishing Connections: People with and Without Disabilities Together at Mealtime
Karin Melberg Schwier and Erin Schwier Stewart
Paul H. Brookes Publishing Co. Baltimore, 2005
A feast of insight into the art of dining and hospitality.

Building Communities from the Inside Out: a Path Towards Finding and Mobilizing a Community's Assets
John McKnight and John Kretzmann
We continue to model our work at PLAN on John McKnight's analysis and insights. You can download a pdf copy by searching Google for this title.

The Careless Society
John McKnight
New York: Basic Books, 1995
This represents the best of John's writing. Inspired by the CBC radio series, "Community and Its Counterfeits." John and his writings are a major inspiration to Al Etmanski.

The Church of 80% Sincerity
David Roche
A Perigee Book, New York, 2008
This is a funny, honest, and irresistible glimpse into everyone's inner beauty and worth.

Community: The Structure of Belonging
Peter Block
Berret-Koehler Publishers, Inc.; San Francisco, 2008
Peter eloquently and elegantly explains how belonging is the path by which communities can emerge out of fragmentation.

In the Company of Others
Claude Whitmyer, editor
Revised by Cathy Ludlum and the Communitas Team
New York: Jeremy Tarcher, 1993
This is a compilation of writings on the art of community development and building community connections.

The Company of Others: Stories of Belonging
Sandra Shields and David Campion
Vancouver, The PLAN Institute, 2005

Crossing The River: Creating a Conceptual Revolution in Community and Disability

David Schwartz

Cambridge, Mass.: Brookline Books, 1992

The best description from an American point of view on the new way of thinking—or the paradigm shift–in social services for people with disabilities.

The Diving Bell and the Butterfly

Jean-Dominique Bauby

London, Fourth Estate, 1997

Recently made into a compelling and thoughtful movie.

Down Stairs That Are Never Your Own: Supporting People with Developmental Disabilities in Their Own Homes

John O'Brien and Connie Lyle O'Brien

Visit http://thechp.syr.edu/rsa.htm

This is a good overview of alternatives to group homes and the conceptual shift that will be required in order to achieve widespread home ownership or rental accommodation for people with disabilities.

Facing Death, Embracing Life

David Kuhl, M.D.

Doubleday Canada, 2006

A sensitive and all encompassing guide for those living with a terminal illness and for those who care about them.

Four Walls of My Freedom

Donna Thompson

London UK: McArthur & Co.

Donna Thompson reflects on issues of inclusion through the lens of her personal family experience.

From Behind The Piano—The Building of Judith Snow's Unique Circle of Friends

Jack Pearpoint

Toronto: Inclusion Press, 1990

This is the book to read if you want to learn more about Judith Snow, an amazing human being.

Getting to Maybe: How the World is Changed

Frances Westley, Brenda Zimmerman, and Michael Patton

Toronto, Random House, 2006

PLAN's story is one of many used to illustrate a new approach to changing the world.

The Healing Web—Social Networks and Human Survival

Marc Pilisak and Susan Hillier Parks

University Press of New England, 1986

This book will give you all the theory behind the importance of social networks. In our opinion, it is a classic and a must read for anyone who wants to dig a bit deeper.

How to Change the World—Social Entrepreneurs and Power of New Ideas

David Bornstein

New York, Oxford University Press, 2004

This book tells the stories of people who have both changed lives and found ways to change the world.

Mind/Body Health: The Effects of Attitudes, Emotions and Relationships (3rd Edition)

Keith J. Karren, Brent Q. Hafen, Kathryn J. Frandsen, Lee Smith

This is a very good book for introducing body/mind health issues.

The Myth of Ability
The End of Ignorance
John Mighton

Vintage Canada, Toronto

John's writings honour and apply to every child. He pays attention to how kids pay attention, captures their imagination, and enlarges their self-confidence. Now available in e-book format.

On Equilibrium
John Ralston Saul

Toronto, Penguin Books, 2001

John is PLAN's Patron, collaborator, and intellectual inspiration. The sections on Imagination and Intuition are thoughtful; they validate what formal systems ignore or discard.

One Candle Power—Seven Principles that Enhance the Lives of People with Disabilities and their Communities
Pat Beeman, George Ducharme, and Beth Mount's original work on Circles brought together, revised, and updated.

Toronto: Inclusion Press, www.inclusion.com. A classic!

Path & MAPS Handbook: Person Centered Ways to Build Community
John O'Brien, Jack Pearpoint & Lynda Kahn (2010)

This handbook reflects what we have learned since Jack and John and Marsha wrote the Path Workbook in 1995. It provides a stronger foundation for PATH and MAPS by connecting person-centred planning to the work of community building. It is a supplement, not a replacement for the existing books.

PATH: Planning Possible Positive Futures
Marsha Forest, Jack Pearpoint, and John O'Brien

Toronto: Inclusion Press

We like this one a lot. It's a practical planning process that provides a good way of stepping out of the day-to-day and allowing your heart and mind to soar. It also provides an excellent structure for strategic and future planning. Visit www.inclusion.com.

Pathways to Inclusion: Building a New Story with People and Community
John Lord and Peggie Hutchison

Concord Ontario, Captus Press, 2007

This is an examination of various perspectives on disability. John and Peggie provide insightful discussion on the current need for social innovation to move vulnerable citizens from areas of exclusion to social inclusion.

Peace Begins With Me
Ted Kuntz

Coquitlam, 2005

Ted is a Past President of PLAN. This best selling book inspires people from all around the world. Visit www.peacebeginswithme.ca.

Reaching Out
Nancy Rother

PLAN, 2004

This is a portrait of facilitated social network development across Canada. Filled with the wisdom of individuals, families, and facilitators from all walks of life, it is one of the clearest, most practical guides you will find on facilitating networks.

Roots of Empathy—Changing the World Child by Child

Mary Gordon

Thomas Allen Publishers, Toronto, 2005

Mary is a spirited colleague whose work brings babies into classrooms to foster empathy, reduce aggression, and increase tolerance.

Sleepwalking Among the Camels: New and Selected Poems

Tom Konyves

Muses Co., 1994

A collection of poems including Lost and Found.

Slow Dance: A Story of Stroke, Love and Disability

Bonnie Sherr Klein

Toronto, Knopf Canada 1998

Support Circles: the heart of the matter

Forest, M., Pearpoint, J. & Snow, J.

Inclusion News, 1996

What's Really Worth Doing and How To Do It—A Book for People Who Love Someone Labelled Disabled

Judith Snow

Toronto: Inclusion Press, 1994

Words of wisdom and inspiration from one of the wisest.

The World We Want—Virtue, Vice and The Good Citizen

Mark Kingwell

Toronto, Viking, 2000

Mark's writing on justice provides a thoughtful framework for a new theory of citizenship that includes people with disabilities and others whose contributions have been ignored.

Films and Videos

And Then Came John—The Story of John McGough

A video by Telesis Productions, Mendocino, California

This remains one of our favorites. It's a true story of an artist, who happens to have Down syndrome, and the love that emanates from his connections in the community.

Best Boy

Ira Wohl

This film won an academy award several years back. It's a true story in which the director filmed the process of his cousin, a middle-aged man with a disability, leaving home. There is a companion follow-up documentary as well. You can find it at specialty video stores or libraries.

MY LIFE, MY CHOICE Personal Stories, Struggles and Successes with Person Directed Living

Parashoot Productions Inc.

Inclusion Press (www.inclusion.com)

My Life, My Choice profiles seven adults with disabilities living Person Directed lives in Windsor, Ontario, Canada. Rather than relying on a limited number of programs and services to direct their lives, their futures are in their own hands.

REVEL IN THE LIGHT:
The Story of Rebecca Beayni

www.rebeccabeayni.com

Masterworks Productions

Rebecca is a woman whose openness to life touches and stirs those in the world around her. This is a testament to love and family and the amazing mystery of hope. This DVD is for families, friends, and individuals with disabilities as well as professionals and community members who wish to create a better world for all.

SHAMELESS: the Art of Disability

A film by Bonnie Sherr Klein

Art, activism, and disability are the starting point for what unfolds as a funny and intimate portrait of five surprising individuals.

The Ties That Bind

Force Four Entertainment Inc.

National Film Board of Canada, 2006

A documentary film about Chris Jordan, his family, and PLAN. There is a companion resource guide in both English and French. This DVD is for all families worried about the future well-being of their relatives with disabilities.

PLAN collaborators

www.abcdinstitute.org This is the home of John McKnight's Asset Based Community Development Institute.

www.abilities.ca This is the website for the Canadian Abilities Association which includes the talented Ray Cohen's many important initiatives such as Access Guide Canada and the award winning Abilities magazine.

www.appartenance-belonging.org Appartenance-Belonging is about the living ties that connect us to each other, to our families, our communities, our country, our beliefs, our earth, our universe. It is about all forms of life.

www.ashoka.ca This is a global fellowship of social entrepreneurs. Al Etmanski was one of the first two Canadians selected to be part of this prestigious network.

www.cdss.ca The positive communications and strong ethical stances make the Canadian Down Syndrome Society a leading advocacy organization.

http://chance.unh.edu/ The Center for Housing and New Community Economics. Chance is dedicated to increasing access to integrated, affordable and accessible housing.

www.communityworks.info This is the website of David and Faye Wetherow, social inventors, trainers, and consultants.

www.depts.washington.edu Michael J. Guralnick, Ph.D, Director of the Center on Human Development and Disability, Professor of Psychology and Pediatrics, University of Washington, Seattle, Washington USA.

www.fieldnotes.ca This is the website of Sandra Shields and David Campion. This talented couple have dedicated their writing, photographic and artistic talent to economic and social justice issues.

www.ilcanada.ca This is the umbrella organization for the Independent Living movement in Canada and a network of Independent Living Centres.

www.in-control.org.uk This website is testimony to the power of families and individuals with disabilities. In Control led the campaign for direct funding or self-directed support for the elderly and people with disabilities.

www.inclusion.com This is the website of Inclusion Press International and the great work of Jack Pearpoint, Lynda Kahn, Cathy Hollands, and the late, esteemed Marsha Forest.

www.larche.ca L'Arche is PLAN's closest collaborator, embodying and exemplifying the work of their founder Jean Vanier. It is worth subscribing to A Human Future, a quarterly electronic publication featuring thought provoking interviews with outstanding Canadians.

www.mcconnellfoundation.ca This website is the home of the progressive JW McConnell Family Foundation and long-time supporter of PLAN and the PLAN Institute.

www.normemma.com This website links to the talented, inspirational and humorous team of Norman Kunc and Emma Van der Klift who provide keynote addresses, workshops, and training in the areas of inclusive education and disability rights.

www.qualitymall.org This is a website where you can find free information about person-centered supports for people with developmental disabilities. Each of the "Mall Stores" has departments you can look through to learn about positive practices that help people with developmental disabilities live, work and participate in our communities and improve the quality of their supports.

www.tamarackcommunity.ca This website is full of resources and practical advice for community engagement, community organizing, and convening.

Relevant organizations

Alberta Aids to Daily Living
www.seniors.alberta.ca/aadl
Offers partial subsidy for various technical supports (for example, wheelchairs and prostheses) to help individuals live as independent as possible.

Alberta Association for Community Living
www.aacl.org
The Alberta Association for Community Living (AACL) is a family based, non-profit federation that advocates on behalf of children and adults with developmental disabilities and their families.

Alberta Civil Liberties Research Centre
http://www.ucalgary.ca/uofc/Others/aclrc/
Its mission is to promote awareness among Albertans about civil liberties and human rights through research and education.

Alberta Income for the Severely Handicapped (AISH)
www.seniors.alberta.ca/aish
(or Alberta RITE Operator 310-0000 and ask to be connected free of charge)
The Assured Income for the Severely Handicapped (AISH) program provides financial and health-related assistance to eligible adults with a disability.

Autism Society of Alberta

www.autismsocietyalberta.org

Autism Society Alberta (ASA) exists to support local groups run by families and individuals with ASD; to facilitate communication and collaboration amongst these groups in Alberta; to work together on regional and provincial issues; and to speak on behalf of families and individuals affected by Autism Spectrum Disorders (ASD) at the provincial level. Autism Spectrum Disorder (ASD) includes Autism, Asperger's Syndrome, Pervasive Developmental Disabilities Not Otherwise Specified (PDD-NOS) and Rett's Syndrome. People connected to other disabilities are also welcome to join. From this site you can access regional chapters.

Calgary Community Living Society

www.cclscalgary.com

A grassroots family association committed to creating inclusive communities, CCLS provides advocacy, information, and support to families and individuals with developmental disabilities; offers family to family support and networking; advocates for community inclusive practices and policies; represents the interests of families in the Calgary area; and works collaboratively with other organizations who share common values.

Canadian Down Syndrome Society

www.cdss.ca

The Canadian Down Syndrome Society is a national non-profit organization providing information, advocacy, and education about Down syndrome. The CDSS supports self-advocates, parents, and families through all stages of life.

Canada Mortgage and Housing Corporation — Prairie and Territories Region

www.cmhc-schl.gc.ca/en/corp/cous/cous

For information about services specifically for persons with disabilities such as non-refundable medical expenses, tax credits, renovations, and so on.

Canada Revenue Agency

www.cra-arc.gc.ca/disability/

For information about services specifically for persons with disabilities such as non-refundable medical expenses, tax credits, renovations, and so on.

Canadian Mental Health

www.cmha.ca

The Canadian Mental Health Association is a nation-wide, charitable organization that promotes the mental health of all and supports the resilience and recovery of people experiencing mental illness.

Canadian Society for Rare Disorders

www.raredisorders.ca

CORD is Canada's national network for organizations representing all those with rare disorders. CORD provides a strong common voice to advocate for health policy and a healthcare system that works for those with rare disorders.

Cerebral Palsy Association in Alberta

www.cpalberta.com

CPAA serves people of all abilities through: individual and family support programs; information and referral services; employment training; sport, social and recreation programs; community and government relations; educational and awareness activities.

Children's Link Society

www.childrenslink.ca

The Children's Link Society is a family-centred, community-based, central access point of information for families of children with special needs in Calgary and area. Its resource service does not duplicate but enhances existing services within the Calgary and area.

FASD Support and Resources in Alberta

www.fasd.typepad.com/

This site lists services, supports, and resources specifically for families and other caregivers of children, youth, and adults affected by Fetal Alcohol Spectrum Disorder (FASD) in Edmonton, Calgary and other regions of Alberta.

The Gateway Association

www.gatewayassociation.ca

Gateway is a family resource centre that provides education, family support, and mentorship in the Edmonton area. Its mission is to assist the community to understand intellectual disabilities.

Persons with Developmental Disabilities (PDD)

www.seniors.alberta.ca/pdd/contact/

The PDD Program funds, monitors, and evaluates the provision of specific services for adult Albertans with developmental disabilities. These services supplement the support of family, friends, and community members and assist the individual in living as independently as possible in the community. There are six regional PDD community boards, which are agents of the Crown. These boards work with individuals, their representatives and families, and service providers to deliver services throughout Alberta.

Premier's Council on the Status of Persons with Disabilities

www.seniors.alberta.ca/premierscouncil/

The Premier's Council on the Status of Persons with Disabilities is to advise, report to, and make recommendations to the Government of Alberta on matters relating to the opportunity for full and equal participation of persons with disabilities.

Office of the Public Guardian

www.seniors.alberta.ca/opg/

(or Alberta RITE Operator 310-0000 and ask to be connected free of charge)

The Office of the Public Guardian (OPG) provides decision-making mechanisms for individuals who are unable to make personal, non-financial decisions for themselves. The OPG does this through the *Personal Directives Act*, *the Adult Guardianship and Trusteeship Act* and the *Mental Health Act*. The OPG also administers the Personal Directives Registry and the Adult Guardianship and Trusteeship Registry.

The Public Trustee

http://justice.alberta.ca/programs_services/public_trustee (or Alberta RITE Operator 310-0000 and ask to be connected free of charge)

The Public Trustee is appointed by the Government of Alberta under the *Public Trustee Act* to protect and manage the financial interests of vulnerable Albertans. The trust administrators, lawyers, taxation officers, auditors, and support staff in the Office of the Public Trustee act on behalf of people with mental disabilities, administer the estates of deceased persons, and protect the property interests of minors.

Special Needs Association for Parents and Siblings (Foothills SNAPS)

www.foothillssnaps.com

This non-profit organization serves the Foothills area of Alberta including Nanton, High River, Black Diamond, Claresholm, MD of Foothills, Okotoks, DeWinton, Longview, Millarville, Turner Valley, Blackie and Red Deer Lake. Its mission is to create fully inclusive communities by enhancing the lives of individuals with special needs through family support.

Special Kidz — Alberta Premier Special Needs Resource Guide

www.special-kidz-canada.com

A one-stop information centre that will have what your family needs.

Ups and Downs Society

www.upsdowns.org

Ups and Downs is a registered, not-for-profit, organization for individuals with Down syndrome, their friends and families. Founded in 1984 by a group of concerned parents, Ups and Downs now provides a wide variety of service, programs and activities for its members, and volunteer opportunities for Calgarians.

Upside Down in LA Lethbridge Down Syndrome Family Support Group

Contact info: upsidedowninla@hotmail.com.

PLAN and PLAN affiliates

Al Etmanski's blog
www.aletmanski.com

Planned Lifetime Advocacy Network Calgary (The Road Ahead Society)
www.plancalgary.ca

Lethbridge Association for Community Living
www.lacl.ca

Planned Lifetime Advocacy Networks Edmonton (PLAN Edmonton)
www.planedmonton.ca

Planned Lifetime Advocacy Network (PLAN Vancouver)
www.plan.ca

Tyze Personal Networks
www.tyze.ca

PLAN Institute for Citizenship and Disability
www.planinstitute.ca

RDSP Resource Centre

We know you think about the future, if not for yourself, then for those you love. You want tomorrow to be a little better, a little more secure than today. The RDSP is a powerful way for people with disabilities to save for the future. We started the RDSP Resource Centre to help you use an RDSP to create a brighter tomorrow.

If you have a prolonged impairment as a result of a disability, illness or medical condition, you may qualify to open an RDSP. Our goal is to help you qualify for the disability tax credit, get your RDSP open, and start saving.

Visit our website **www.rdspresource.ca** or contact us at **1-855-773-7377** for a free RDSP Eligibility Assessment.

In partnership with PLAN.

PLAN Books and Products

PLAN and PLAN Institute for Caring Citizenship offer products for sale. Please see below for a list of items and a brief description. To order, please visit **www.plan.ca** or **www.planinstitute.ca.**

The Company of Others

The Company of Others, a creative collaboration by author Sandra Shields and photographer David Campion, uniquely captures the spirit and significance of personal networks. Compelling stories and photographs lead the reader on an intimate journey into the lives of five individuals—with no connection to one other and little in common, except in one respect: each person is at the centre of an active social "circle"—a network of caring friends and family whose lives are enriched by the relationship they share. An extraordinary and moving book about the transformative power of family and community.

A Good Life

A Good Life for You and Your Relative With a Disability is an inspirational guide to rethinking disability and the value of people with disability in a caring society. It provides families, caregivers and those worried about the well-being of people with disabilities with insights, stories of inspiration, and practical advice. It offers a step by step guide to creating a plan for the future which provides for the safety, security, and well-being of people with disabilities.

Peace of Mind (CD)

The *Peace of Mind* CD-ROM is a practical and loving guide to help you plan for the future of your relative with a disability. It combines personal stories, testimonials, tips, and step-by-step worksheets to get you started on your path to peace of mind.

Reaching Out

Reaching Out by Nancy Rother, is a portrait of facilitated social network development across Canada. Filled with the wisdom of individuals, families, and facilitators from all walks of life, it is one of the clearest, most practical guides you will find on facilitating networks.

The Ties That Bind (DVD)

a National Film Board of Canada production

In *The Ties That Bind* award winning documentary, filmmaker John Ritchie takes a first hand look at a family's struggle to let go, when every instinct compels them to hang on. Ritchie follows the Jordon family—Kathleen, Bill, Chris and his two siblings—for almost three years. The result in an extraordinarily intimate film that reveals, with raw emotion and surprising humour, the complexity around one young man's transition toward a more independent life.

Peace Begins With Me

In *Peace Begins With Me*, Ted Kuntz shares the story of his journey of making peace with his son's disabilities. It is a journey through darkness to a life that is now filled with peace, joy, and happiness. At the core of Ted's message are simple yet powerful strategies that enable all of us to experience more peace and joy and create a life more of our choosing. A must read!